Buckingh

DAVID KIDD-HEWITT

COUNTRYSIDE BOOKS
NEWBURY BERKSHIRE

First published 2005
© David Kidd-Hewitt, 2005

COUNTRYSIDE BOOKS
3 Catherine Road
Newbury, Berkshire

To view our complete range of books,
please visit us at
www.countrysidebooks.co.uk

ISBN 1 85306 929 9
EAN 978 185306 929 1

For my heroes: Jan, Rach and Paul

Designed by Peter Davies, Nautilus Design
Produced through MRM Associates Ltd., Reading
Printed by Arrowsmith, Bristol

CONTENTS

Foreword

T he county of Buckinghamshire has seen many heroes over the centuries, some recognised as such but many more the 'unsung' heroes of their time. To call someone a hero is also a very personal decision, there is no agreed and undisputed group of people gathered under such a title. Consequently, for all kinds of reasons, which I hope become clear as each of their stories unfolds, this is very much my collection of Buckinghamshire heroes.

Roald Dahl begins our hero's journey from his village of Great Missenden and, in so doing, opens up a world of quite remarkable personal endeavour and perseverance amid disproportionate encounters with tragedy. This world-famous children's author has a spectacular non-fiction story of his own to tell. His story also reveals an unsung hero as integral not only to his family's well-being at a critical time, but to many thousands of people across the years: she is local villager, Valerie Eaton Griffith.

Station X then brings to our attention heroes galore in the stark, crucial and complex world of war-time code breaking – these are the hidden heroes of Bletchley Park. Follow the tense race to crack the German military codes during war-torn Britain. A classic wartime film hero takes up our focus next, as we visit the story of one of Buckinghamshire's favourite local celebrities, the much missed, Sir John Mills.

The world has revered our next hero – the first woman to receive the British Order of Merit – Florence Nightingale. This is the other side of that remarkable woman, working in north Buckinghamshire with another pioneering hero from Buckingham, Dr George De'Ath, who is very much one of the county's unsung heroes.

Why is Sir William Borlase's Grammar School in Marlow, sporting a commemorative plaque to Ken 'Snakehips' Johnson? Find out about this fascinating man and why Buckinghamshire

FOREWORD

and Marlow, in particular, embrace him as an adopted hero.

Selflessness under personal adversity is a rare commodity and when it involves a young lad barely into his teens, it is heart-warming . Prestwood's Thomas Ball both warms your heart whilst pulling at its strings – his story reveals a hero of a generous disposition for one so young.

John Hampden takes us back to the cut and thrust of earlier times in the county – a fighter for democracy and a hero of traditional qualities, battling for the people and for justice.

Also battling in another way was the founder of Wycombe Abbey School, Dame Frances Dove, educationalist and High Wycombe's one woman 'whirlwind'; a unique woman in her energy, inspiration and practical delivery of a whole range of health and educational facilities for the town.

Then, from an attic in Olney, some of the world's most famous lines were penned by the curate there, John Newton. *Amazing Grace* gives us an insight into a remarkable period in Olney's history – who is the hero here? The man? The hymn? Or the villagers?

We return to the Great Missenden area to relax in the comfortable presence of one of the country's favourite actors and much admired local celebrity, Geoffrey Palmer OBE. His contribution to his profession was rewarded in the 2005 Honours List and, when you read his engaging story, you might feel that it was a tad overdue.

I do hope you enjoy meeting my Buckinghamshire heroes.

David Kidd-Hewitt

ACKNOWLEDGEMENTS

This book could not have been completed without the generosity of so many willing to assist in its compilation, particularly when the story is their own. Heartfelt thanks go to: Geoffrey Palmer OBE who gave me so much of his time; Elaine Ball for Tom's story; Ron Compton for his memories of his fellow class mate, Ken 'Snakehips' Johnson; also to Patrick Gazard, Head of Music and Lee Mumbray-Williams, Librarian at Sir William Borlase's Grammar School, Marlow, for their invaluable asssistance. Also to the generosity and expertise of Andy Simons, Social History Curator, the Modern British Collections at the British Library. Thank you Valerie Eaton Griffith for telling me of your times with Roald Dahl and Patricia Neal. Many thanks to Liz Whittingham, Collections Manager, Sue Davies, Director at the Roald Dahl Museum and Story Centre, plus Amanda Conquy, Managing Director, and Dominic Gregory, Manager at Dahl & Dahl Ltd. Extracts from Roald Dahl's works are by kind permission of Dahl & Dahl. More thanks to Karen Parr, Museum Administrator at the Cowper and Newton Museum, and to Sam Hearn and Roy Bailey of the John Hampden Society, plus Michael Hillman and Robert Chamber's *Book of Days*. As always, thanks to the extraordinarily helpful folk at the Centre for Buckinghamshire Studies and once more to Alison Heath, Archivist at Wycombe Abbey School. To Jo Tiddy, Heritage Officer at Wycombe District Council and also to Rita and Peter Strudwick.

Special thanks to Jan Baldwin for permission to use her photograph of Roald Dahl in his writing hut, and to Steve Cohen and Sally Swift of the *Bucks Free Press* for arranging the photograph of Sir John Mills. To Ann Cotterell of Northway Publications for the 'Snakehips' image, Sir William Borlase's Grammar School and Mrs Frances Chouffot for Ken's school cricket photo and to Robert Breakwell, Appeals Director of The Iain Rennie Hospice at Home for Geoffrey Palmer's charity wristband photograph.

1

Roald Dahl (1916–1990)

'I only have child power'

High over the Buckinghamshire village of Great Missenden, the morning sun casts its glow across the sloping, grassy churchyard that dips down towards the early bustle of the school run and commuter traffic. Shadows slide across flowers, toys and tributes of all kinds that mark the memories and emotions of many whose loved ones now lie untroubled by the frantic scrambling in the valley below. Extraordinarily large footprints lead off into the morning dew from the comfort of a warmly weathered circular seat inscribed with the names of Olivia, Tessa, Theo, Ophelia, Lucy, Neisha, Charlotte and Lorina.

Whoever the visitor was, their stride was as gigantic as their footprints. Closer examination reveals that the footprints are cast in stone and not, after all, transitory clues left by an early morning visitor paying their respects. Follow the foot prints down, vainly trying to match the stride, and you will reach a polished granite memorial marked like many others with a small container of silk flowers.

Before you can read the inscription, you will, as likely as not, notice this memorial is not, after all, like many others. For this smooth, dark, green surface set into the gentle slope is scattered with an assortment of sweets: two damp cellophane wrappers revealing love hearts; a tube of Smarties; some chocolate bars in various stages of disintegration; a toffee or two; and perhaps a note accompanying one or more of the sugary gifts. For these sweets are both gifts and memorials – an ever-changing tributary collage created by the young (and sometimes not so young), who revere and continue to enjoy the everlasting magic and adventure they have been given by the man who now rests in peace in this parish churchyard. The footsteps, guiding the way, belong to the Big Friendly Giant, and they halt almost as if he were standing there, gazing at the inscription carved deeply into the stone:

**ROALD
DAHL
13 SEPTEMBER
1916
23 NOVEMBER
1990**

By the Giant's side those, who choose, can see little orphan Sophie who shared the BFG's adventures which began in this very village of Great Missenden.

'What happens when a giant dies?' Sophie asked. 'Giants is never dying,' the BFG answered. 'Sometimes and quite suddenly, a giant is disappearing and nobody is ever knowing where he goes to. But mostly us giants is simply going on and on like whiffsy time-twiddlers.'

Whatever brief moments of imaginative flight one may enjoy, courtesy of the genius of Roald Dahl, when you take time to look behind this most loved, successful and well-known children's writer; when you engage in a modest amount of 'whiffsy time-twiddling', you discover you are in the presence of a true Buckinghamshire hero.

Before the literary fame which was to transform his life and bring so much reading pleasure to children and adults everywhere, Roald Dahl had already proved himself an extraordinarily intricate, engaging, courageous and inventive

ROALD DAHL (1916–1990)

character. Frighteningly diverse, he was able to turn his hand to almost anything he cared to and certainly always able to take control of the most difficult personal situations. Roald Dahl had the drive to pluck and push solutions through the darkest tunnels and out into the light.

To explain this side of Roald Dahl, we need to see him, not as a world-famous author, the lone figure in his writing hut, sleeping bag around his legs, board across his lap, yellow pad and sharpened pencils at the ready, but as a perceptive inventor, philanthropist and, when the occasion warranted it, a tenacious fighter and deeply affectionate family man. It is only then that all the rest makes sense, when his legacy is fleshed out beyond the confines of the book cover and film script.

Roald Dahl in his writing hut. (courtesy Jan Baldwin)

BUCKINGHAMSHIRE HEROES

Before we reach this 'other' Roald Dahl, and indeed, Buckinghamshire, we need to get to know the boy born in Llandaff, Wales, on 13th September 1916. Harald Dahl and Sofie Hesselberg from Norway had married in 1911. Harald was the co-owner of a ship-broking business in Cardiff. Roald had four sisters but, as a three-year-old, was faced with two family deaths when his eight-year-old sister Astri died of appendicitis and his father died of pneumonia, both in 1920. His mother, Sofie, was so precious to him. The importance of being loved and not being alone was a theme that was to occur frequently in his career as an author. He was always clear that his mother '. . . was the absolute primary influence on my own life. She had a crystal-clear intellect and a deep interest in almost everything under the sun. She was the matriarch, the *materfamilias* and her children radiated round her like planets round a sun.' (*Memories with Food*, 1991, pp 65/6)

Change matriarch to patriarch and we can begin to see in this observation an indication of what Roald himself would become to his own family. His intellect, fired by a vivid imagination, would lead not only to fantastic tales, but to Dahl the inventor, and is beautifully illustrated in the opening to his book of childhood and adolescent memories entitled *My Year*, (1993):

'When I was a little boy, I had a tiny boat made of tin (there was no plastic in those days) which had a very small clockwork motor inside it, and I used to play with it while I was having my bath. One day the tiny boat developed a leak in its hull and it filled with water and sank.

For many weeks after that, I would lie in my bath worrying about whether my own skin would develop a leak in it just as the little boat's hull had done, and I felt certain my body would fill with water and I would sink and die. But it never happened and I marvelled at the watertightness of the skin that covered my body.' (*My Year*, 1993, p5)

ROALD DAHL (1916–1990)

◆◆

This was a boy who, aged nine, created a Conker Practising Machine, capable of taking on six conkers at a time. A boy who, excited by his Christmas gift of a Meccano outfit, decided not to follow the many examples of what marvels you can construct, but to create something that had never been built before and believe me, this, by any stretch of the Meccano imagination had not been built before (nor since I would have thought). By stretching a wire from the roof of his house, over the top of a footpath to a nearby fence (around 100 yards), he was able to use the special grooved wheel and metal struts to make a device capable of speeding down this sloping wire with a hanging cargo of five used Heinz soup cans – cans now filled to the brim with water. A string leading back to his eager hand would tilt the water out when jerked and, ideally, when passing over innocent pedestrians on the footpath.

'Soon two ladies dressed in tweed skirts and jackets and each wearing a hat, came strolling up the path with a revolting little Pekinese dog on a lead. I knew I had to time this carefully, so, when they were very nearly but not quite directly under the wire, I let my chariot go. Down she went, making a wonderful screeching-humming noise as the metal wheel ran down the wire and the string ran through my fingers at great speed.

Bombing from a height is never easy. I had to guess when my chariot was directly over the target, and when that moment came, I jerked the string. The chariot stopped dead and the tins swung upside down and all the water tipped out. The ladies, who had halted and looked up on hearing the rushing noise of my chariot overhead, caught the cascade of water full in their faces. It was tremendous. A bulls-eye first time.' (*My Year*, 1993, p63)

This one priceless example contains many of the traits of the adult Roald Dahl we are about to uncover: inventive intellect, doing something no one else has done, practical joking, perceptive timing, risk taking and bombing.

He survived a tough boarding school education, fraught with bullying but glistening with sporting success, particularly boxing. It seems a contradiction that this tall 'soft-faced' lad who could box and play a good game of cricket and was excellent at squash, would become such a bullies' victim. But for bullies read 'Boazers' – these were 'career' bullies, part of the English public school system which thrived on the rules and rituals of 'fagging'. Perhaps we could even credit this bizarre system for encouraging his mind to ponder and wander, whilst warming the Boazers' frost-covered outside toilet seat. He recalls Boazer Wilberforce's pearls of wisdom on taking charge of a satisfactorily winter-warmed seat prepared by Dahl, 'Some Fags have cold bottoms, and some have hot ones. I only use hot-bottomed Fags to heat my bog seat. I won't forget you.'

What we can credit to his time at Repton is a love and amazing knowledge of chocolate. Inside the complex imagination of that teenage boy, who knows exactly when the seed was sown for the later creation of one of his most famous literary and film successes, *Charlie and the Chocolate Factory*? The famous Cadbury chocolate factory, in an ingenious marketing initiative for its day, would send new chocolate bar creations for the boys of Repton to taste, test and comment on. Roald Dahl had found his forte and recalls a dream, 'I used to picture a long white room like a laboratory with pots of chocolate and fudge and all sorts of other delicious fillings bubbling away on the stoves, while men and women in white coats moved between the bubbling pots, tasting and mixing and concocting wonderful new inventions.' (*Boy*, 1984, p134)

In this dream Roald would go on to create the most miraculous chocolate taste in the world. From that time onwards he kept his love of chocolate honed and always maintained that school history lessons would be better served by teaching the names, not of kings and queens and their reigns, but the names of chocolate bars and the dates they were created.

ROALD DAHL (1916–1990)

The clues are steadily emerging to understand this man's remarkable persona. We need to fast forward to two significant parts of his life before we can reach our Buckinghamshire destination of Great Missenden. A man of great practicality and adventure, Dahl opted for a real challenge rather than reading for a degree and at seventeen joined the Public Schools Exploring Expedition to Newfoundland. Here was adventure, excitement and danger, wandering into uncharted territory, blank spaces on existing maps – perhaps he might find a gold mine, he thought. He didn't, and in September 1934, aged eighteen, he joined the oil giant, Shell. Languishing in the London office, he was frustrated knowing that others were exploring the world on Shell's behalf. His patience was rewarded, however, when after four years of tolerating this (and many chocolate bars later – he turned their wrappings into a giant silver ball, a surreal calendar of being office-bound), he was posted to Dar es Salaam. Camera always by his side, Dahl used the opportunity to store up experiences that would come tumbling out later on in his writing days. It is no coincidence that the tarantula in a friend's shoe and the green mamba sliding across the floor would be fodder to his hugely successful adult writings such as *Tales of the Unexpected*.

Less unexpected was the declaration of war in 1939. Now 23, Dahl immediately joined the Royal Air Force in Nairobi. Here, with difficulty, he bent his lanky frame into the cockpit of a Tiger Moth and learnt to fly over the Kenyan Highlands. His Meccano bombing ingenuity as a boy now saw him flying over the Iraqi desert, no empty soup cans filled with water this time, but with real weapons as he spent six months learning to shoot, navigate and dive-bomb. Later, trying to land an unfamiliar plane – a Gloster Gladiator – for re-fuelling, he crash-landed and was engulfed in flames. Roald Dahl had fractured his skull but managed to escape serious burn injuries. He was, however, temporarily blinded and remained swollen and in great pain for

*Roald Dahl in tropical RAF uniform,
Haifa 1941 (© RDNL)*

some time. With characteristic determination, he pushed to fly again with the now much depleted 80 Squadron and this time he would see action and emerge a hero. During April, 1941, flying a Hurricane, he took part in raids over Athens against the invading Germany military, resulting in dogfights during which he succeeded in downing several enemy aircraft. Dahl is credited in the official records of having shot down six enemy aircraft which, in a hectic period of five weeks solid fighting, was of heroic status. He no doubt would have notched up more but blinding headaches from his earlier crash saw him reluctantly invalided out. Here were more experiences for the author-inside waiting to emerge.

Following his heroic feats as a pilot, Dahl became bored. His imagination required feeding and so began an intense interest in collecting modern art and whilst his boredom was staved through this new passion and the celebrity network it encompassed, a new posting came through. Dahl was appointed Assistant Air Attaché to the British Embassy in Washington, a post that would also connect him to the British Intelligence Services. His

BUCKINGHAMSHIRE HEROES

imagination would never go hungry again. Dahl loved Washington and the celebrity party circuit in the States, and women in particular, loved him back. He was an injured fighter pilot hero, young, lanky, handsome, very witty and connected to the secret services, albeit very loosely and he had tales to tell, including his own experiences with gremlins. All RAF pilots were familiar with gremlins. They waited until you were airborne and then out they would gleefully come, as this extract from *Song of the Gremlins*, attributed to the RAF Photographic Reconnaissance Unit testifies:

> 'White ones will wiggle your wingtips
> Male ones will muddle your maps
> Green ones will guzzle your Glycol
> Females will flutter your flaps
> Pink ones will perch on your perspex
> And dance pirouettes on your prop
> There's a special middle aged Gremlin
> Who'll spin on your stick like a top.'

During this time he became acquainted with the famous novelist C.S Forester of *Captain Hornblower* fame who encouraged Dahl to write about his experiences. The result was his first foray into professional authorship with 'Shot Down Over Libya' which appeared anonymously in the US magazine *Saturday Evening Post* in August 1942.

But Dahl hooked a far bigger fish when his knowledge of gremlins reached the ears of a certain Walt Disney and Hollywood was keen to meet this extraordinary storyteller. *Snow White*, *Pinocchio* and *Fantasia* were to give way to lightweight propaganda and training movies during these war years, but now Disney wanted Dahl's gremlins. Except they weren't Dahl's gremlins; they belonged to the RAF who, to a man, claimed they existed. Gremlin Lore as recounted by Dahl reached the bizarre stage of Disney attempting to confirm actual sightings, descriptions and even accent. It was a masterpiece of a spoof with Dahl pulling as many legs as he could. When Disney's animators at Burbank tried to capture their likeness, Dahl told them,'I am very glad to see that you had no definite views about Gremlins not wearing bowler hats, but their omission in your drawings did cause a little trouble.' Disney titles for the project ranged from 'Gremlin Gambols,' 'Gay Gremlins' and 'We've got Gremlins'.

'Stalky', as Walt Disney called Dahl, was in his element. Living an expenses-paid life in Hollywood and pulling so many legs it's a wonder Burbank didn't collapse. In the event, the film was never made but the story was published as a picture book in 1943 entitled, *Walt Disney: The Gremlins (A Royal Airforce Story by Flight Lieutenant Roald Dahl).*

The author inside had finally made his debut – this was Roald Dahl's first book. He signed with a literary agent and articles came tumbling out for the likes of *Harpers, Cosmopolitan* and *The Ladies Home Journal.*

Dahl was on his way to fame, fortune and Great Missenden but there were many tragedies to overcome on the way.

His mother Sofie had moved from Kent to Buckinghamshire, firstly to Grendon Underwood, then to Grange Farm, Great Missenden, and then to Amersham. Roald settled in at his mother's Grendon home determined to continue as an author. As she moved, Roald moved with her. At the Amersham address and as restless as ever for other interests, he took up greyhound breeding with the local butcher, Claud Taylor. This friendship led to other pastimes such as tickling trout and poaching pheasant. The contrast with Hollywood couldn't have been greater and brought Dahl into the Buckinghamshire village idyll he was to adore for the rest of this life. Sometimes he pretended not to

ROALD DAHL (1916–1990)

enjoy it because that always got a reaction and he thrived on reaction.

As he increased his output of short stories for adults and developed broadcasting contacts with the BBC, he was relentlessly searching for a niche he couldn't quite identify. He also still suffered back pain from his flying accident which would always remain with him. Whilst the author blossomed, there was another passion inside Dahl. Together with an equally passionate, influential, multi-millionaire friend from his Washington days, Charles Marsh, a newspaper and oil tycoon, he created a charitable trust in 1949 called the Public Welfare Foundation. This philanthropic work was originally targeted at 200 needy families in Limehouse, London, to assist the acquisition of education and medical care. Philanthropy continues to flourish in his name under the Roald Dahl Foundation based in Great Missenden, now taking in the whole of the UK and aimed at grants for literacy, and the medical areas of haematology and neurology. The original Public Welfare Foundation, however, was quite an amazing achievement and a tribute to Dahl's caring nature – a trait not often enough realized as it could be swamped by his penetrating, jagged humour and satirical wit. For example, rejecting his friend Marsh's offer of vitamins to give to the poor, Roald is claimed to have said that the poor, 'do not give a f*** for vitamins and do not understand them, they wouldn't eat them even if they were told they were aphrodisiacs.'

At 35, Dahl found himself back in America 'house-sitting' for Charles Marsh and writing hard. His thoughts turned to Buckinghamshire as he wrote a series of local stories under the titles, 'The Ratcatcher' and 'Rummins'. He was, however, receiving his fair share of publishers' rejection letters which displeased him. What did boost his ego and turn his head was his meeting with Hollywood actress, Patricia Neal. It was at a party hosted by Lillian Hellman and she provocatively seated them together. If she had a plan, it worked and they became inseparable and married at Trinity Church, New York in July 1953.

Great Missenden visits followed to meet the Dahl family (Roald's sister Else and her husband John lived nearby) but New York soon claimed them back as it was Patricia's career that was not only based in the States but her fairly substantial income put her as the main wage-earner. Roald was writing but not earning a great deal from his efforts. News of Pat's pregnancy in the summer of 1954 brought them back to Great Missenden where they bought 'Little Whitefield', now famous as Gipsy House. This was to become the life-long base of that other author waiting to emerge – Roald Dahl, children's author.

Meanwhile, as a short-story writer, Dahl was doing exceptionally well; his macabre adult humour scoring a record publishing run for *Someone Like You*. The *New York Times* compared him to Saki and O.Henry, Maupassant and Maugham. To his satisfaction it won a Mystery Writers of America award. On 20th April 1955, Olivia Dahl was born in a Boston hospital and Roald was elated and credited by all who knew him as a doting father. This was to be a hectic period of trans-Atlantic crossings between Great Missenden and New York, whilst Roald continued writing and Pat got back into acting.

At 'Little Whitefield', Dahl looked after Olivia, and, with his practical nature at the fore, built his now famous writing hut in the substantial garden of this lovely Georgian house. This was his writer's 'womb' as he termed it. It was a place to disappear from one world to create another.

He also added the equally famous Gipsy Caravan as a restoration project.

Whilst Dahl's practical side flourished, the creative juices were not delivering at the same pace and depth – he sensed that another direction awaited him but he could not tie it down. Pat was busy in America and Roald was completely absorbed in establishing

ROALD DAHL (1916–1990)

their Great Missenden home, and in particular, a vegetable garden. Onions became his passion. Indeed, vegetables and fruit were one day to be transformed into all kinds of new varieties in children's fictional worlds yet to emerge – quite literally, the seeds were being sown for that moment when snozzcumbers and flying giant peaches would be known the world over.

In April 1957, Tessa Dahl was born in an Oxford hospital. The Dahls were a close family, particularly as Roald's mother, Sofie, now in her seventies was also living nearby in Great Missenden with Roald's sister, Else, and her husband John, at a house called 'Whitefields'. Pat continued to be frantically busy making films and working in live theatre. Elstree to Broadway to Missenden to Hollywood became familiar routes and then once more she was pregnant. By the summer of 1960, baby Theo joined his two sisters.

Dahl's short stories were becoming increasingly popular in England and good reviews led to satisfactory sales. Ironically, American reviewers were becoming less kind to him but the adult public on both sides of the Atlantic loved him and his short story collections such as *Kiss Kiss* flew off the shelves in the early 1960s and began to interest European publishers. Then he put his first step on the bottom rung of what was to be his most successful literary ladder. His early senses that there was another direction, that there was another author inside, now had the necessary catalysts to release the other Roald Dahl. Olivia and Tessa, now five and three, quite literally set their father's imaginative chemistry fizzling and bubbling with joyful, scary stories especially created just for them.

What could be more enthralling at a cosy bedtime moment than when Dad recounted the story of orphan James, escaping his cruel aunts by hiding in a magic peach which falls to earth squashing and killing the pursuing aunts? Then by air and by sea the magic peach takes James and his new-found insect friends to

America, ending up on top on the Empire State Building. He was to turn this bedtime story into the manuscript for *James and the Giant Peach* but first, Roald Dahl and his family were about to enter one of four very long and painful episodes – dark tunnels that required all of Roald's undisputed ingenuity to reach for the light at the end.

On 5th December 1960, Roald was in America working on 'The Centipede Song' for *James and the Giant Peach* when Pat burst into the room with devasting news. Cosy in his pram, four-month-old Theo had been out with his nanny who, tightly clutching Tessa's hand, was on her way to collect Olivia from nursery school whilst Pat enjoyed some shopping. In a sickening instance of carelessness, a taxi-cab had come round the corner as the nanny crossed the road – pram ahead of her.

Shunting and crushing the pram into the side of a bus, Theo was horrifically injured and rushed to hospital. To make matters worse, a second instance of carelessness occurred when a nurse overdosed this frail and seriously injured baby with an anticonvulsant which had to be pumped back out. Theo hung on to life but developed hydrocephalus which created a build-up of cerebrospinal fluid pressure to his brain.

At this stage, understandably, 99.9% of parents would have to watch and wait whilst the medical experts took charge. Roald represented that point one of a percentage of a parent who could not do that. Although Theo would live, the constant draining of fluid from his brain by a small tube and inefficient shunt valve was not reliable. Any blockages could create blindness and fevers and possibly worse.

Dahl reached into his creative practical depths and, like the boy who exhibited such ingenuity with a meccano set in a fun moment, the adult, in this most serious of times, was determined to re-invent the mechanics of this clumsy technology. As a great organiser, networker and inventor all rolled into one, together

ROALD DAHL (1916–1990)

with Pat, he worked to raise money for Theo's exorbitant medical bills, delivered the finished manuscript for *James and the Giant Peach* and then retreated to the relative safety of Great Missenden. Theo rested at home, the inefficient shunt inside his head of great concern to Roald and Pat as it had to be replaced by invasive surgery eight times over a thirty-month period.

Tessa was enrolled at the local Gateway nursery school and Olivia went to nearby Godstowe, just outside High Wycombe. In these early days of Theo's recovery, Dahl the inventor re-emerged. He remembered the times that he used to go to Amersham to fly model gliders, making the acquaintance of Stanley Wade, a hydraulic engineer, also a keen model plane flyer. This turned Roald's mind to the possibility of working with Stanley on improving the valve technology that was so crucial to Theo, and many others like him. The Great Ormond Street doctor treating Theo, Kenneth Till, shared Dahl's concerns for better technology. Between Wade, Till and Dahl, sketches and ideas flowed as they sat at the kitchen table at 'Little Whitefield', or met in Stanley's machine shop near High Wycombe.

Within little more than a year and a half, they had not only patented the Wade-Dahl-Till Valve, and been featured in the foremost medical journal, *The Lancet*, but had brought it out as a working product on the medical market at cost price, (they all agreed not to take a profit), and it became a world-leader, able to safely relieve conditions such as Theo's. Fortunately, Theo was to get much better over the next few years and no longer needed such a device but many thousands of other children across the world did.

During the early 1960s Pat was happily ensconced in their Buckinghamshire home, now renamed Gipsy House, enjoying village life with her newly-minted children's author, and their three children. The book *James and the Giant Peach*, still only available in the United States, had sold a staggering 6,500 copies

– a great success. Roald's Repton days began to invade his writing hut in the smell, texture and fantasy of chocolate and those bubbling laboratory vats he had dreamt of as a teenager. 'Charlie's Chocolate Boy' which he had already submitted as a work in progress just prior to Theo's accident in New York was now re-titled and revised as *Charlie and the Chocolate Factory*. He was hopeful of even greater success with this new story. But, no sooner out of Theo's tunnel, the family were plunged back again into dark days. An outbreak of measles at Godstowe caught up with Olivia and despite emergency medical care, she died. It was 17th November 1962, and the family mourned her so deeply as she was laid to rest in Little Missenden.

Dahl withdrew into himself and we can never know what torments he endured in his 'writer's womb' and at Olivia's grave-side. Pat was equally devastated but also concerned about Roald's mental condition.

He needed to know that heaven contained dogs for Olivia to be with and not just humans, and sought ecclesiastical advice from the Archbishop of Canterbury, his old Repton headmaster. He was angry not to get the confirmation he sought. Writing children's fiction no longer featured in his thoughts. Pat, on the other hand, needed to be busy, to cope with her mental anguish and she threw herself into as many roles as she could land, both television and film. A year later and Pat was pregnant once more.

Ophelia was born in May 1964. Theo was much better now the shunt had been totally removed, and Roald began story-telling again, this time to Tessa and Theo. The world of children's fiction, however, was soon to taste the wonders of Mr Willy Wonka and his mysterious chocolate factory. *Charlie and the Chocolate Factory* was published in America in September 1964 – the first print run of 10,000 copies sold within four weeks. The second rung of his new ladder had been reached.

Pat's fame had also been growing and her love for their Great

ROALD DAHL (1916–1990)

Missenden home and being with her family made being away in the States difficult for her to sustain. However, her income was substantial compared to Roald's at that time and could not be forfeited. The film *Hud*, with Paul Newman, had the film critics acclaiming her performance for which she received an Oscar. Hollywood was pulling her back. Both Pat and Roald were at new beginnings in terms of international fame and recognition yet, to Dahl's considerable annoyance, UK publishers had still to be persuaded to publish *James and the Giant Peach* or *Charlie and the Chocolate Factory*. By February the following year, there were still no takers for the new Roald Dahl, and the family followed Pat to Hollywood for her latest film role with John Wayne called *Seven Women*. Only Roald and Pat, of course, knew she was pregnant once more but no one could have known about the third, dreadful, dark tunnel ahead.

Only four days into the shoot, she was enjoying sharing bathing Tessa with the family nanny when a thunderbolt of a pain tore through her head. Roald did not hesitate for one moment and immediately contacted the neurosurgeon who had dealt with Theo, Charles Carton. Within the space of that phone call, Pat was unconscious, her body convulsing. In hospital, she murmured, 'Who is in this house? What are the names of the people in this house please?' Then she slipped into a coma. Pat was pregnant and close to death; it was a stark reality.

In all, Pat had suffered three strokes and Carton's team worked through the night to remove the haemorrhaged blood threatening her brain. This operation severed the temporal lobe which controls speech and movement. It was a gamble to save her, but, should she survive, her condition would be a serious one. Survive she did but it took over two agonizing weeks before she came round. Amid the family's unbridled joy at her recovery, her transformation was truly startling.

Wearing an eye patch, unable to speak, unable to move her

right side, her hair cruelly shaved away, her mouth twisted to a slight curl; it was a difficult image to store in place of the real Patricia Neal, Oscar-winning Hollywood actress and mother to her three surviving children. More importantly, she was still pregnant. Roald, the ultimate patriarch came to the fore, and took charge of who could and could not see Pat and set about organizing her recovery because he could not envisage anything other than a full recovery. He would lead them all back into that light at the end of the tunnel once more and that light would be in Buckinghamshire not California.

Great Missenden saw a dejected and depressed Pat. She had lost everything that made her a beautiful Hollywood actress – her looks, her voice, her memory; and her right leg was now encased in a brace.

Roald pushed and prodded her into village walks, conversations and shopping – he was convinced that softly, softly, would not work and to some appeared to be over-zealous, even cruel. Village neighbours were recruited to help Pat learn to read again but of more immediate importance at that time was the safe delivery of her baby. In surgeon's gown and mask, Roald watched the birth of their daughter, Lucy Neal Dahl, on 4th August 1965. Now Lucy was safe and healthy, Roald orchestrated his master plan. He needed to work and to bring in money and to keep his own prediction that Pat would make a full recovery. Luckily work came quickly to Roald in the form of an offer to write the screenplay for a James Bond movie – *You only Live Twice*. Roald took up the challenge.

Village neighbour, Valerie Eaton Griffith, whom he had learnt had recently recovered from a thyroid complaint, received a phone call 'out of the blue' from Roald asking if she would 'work' with Pat. Unclear what 'work' meant in this context, Valerie told me, 'I came down to Gipsy House and there was Pat sitting at the kitchen table staring – the saddest face you've ever seen. I did not know what to do but for some strange reason when Pat saw me walk through the doorway, I knew I was going to help her.'

She couldn't have been more perfect as Pat's saviour. In fact, Valerie worked with Pat for five days a week for the next two years, transforming her abilities to speak and enjoy life once more. From a standing start, another Buckinghamshire hero had emerged during this time. Valerie's experience with Pat not only led to their deep and continuing friendship, but she went on to pioneer the Chest and Heart Association which became the Volunteer Stroke Service that continues to undertake so much invaluable assistance to stroke patients today. Even the present-day aims of the VSS reflect exactly what Valerie had made possible for Pat during those dark days in the mid 1960s, i.e. 'improving quality of life by building confidence and improving morale'. Of Roald, Valerie

Patricia Dahl (left) with Valerie Eaton Griffith at the launch of Valerie's book based on her work with Pat.

recalls, 'I thought it was a magnificent effort, the way he worked and managed Pat and the children – he took over the lot.'

In fact, the ever-inventive Roald arranged for Pat and Valerie to go to Hollywood to make an information film called *Stroke/ Counter Stroke* to show the world that recovering from such a severe set-back can be achieved. Roald had firmly, but safely negotiated their way out from that dreadful tunnel.

The film, *You Only Live Twice*, was a smash and Roald could quite rightly reflect in his script-writing glory and thanks to Valerie, Pat was well enough to take on a film role in early 1968, less than three years since her stroke. It was called *The Subject Was Roses*. Valerie worked with her as script-prompter. Thanks to Pat's talent as an actress and Valerie's sheer hard work on script prompting, Pat was nominated for an Academy Award. In the event her co-star got it, but what an achievement by Pat and Valerie; no award was needed to appreciate that.

Sadly, on 17th November 1967, the anniversary of Olivia's death, Roald's beloved mother, Sofie, died aged 82. Roald himself was in extreme pain from his old plane crash injury and it seemed his ever stalwart spirit was fading. Even he could only take so many knocks.

Chitty Chitty Bang Bang appeared to come to his rescue when his second venture into film script work was commissioned. Was he now on another new rung of the ladder? As it turned out, he wasn't. Script disputes between Roald and the director led to Dahl disowning it.

In fact the next few years were characterized by Dahl pushing to enhance his own film-scripting reputation but finding working with directors often as volatile as himself who had the power to alter and criticize his work, a major irritant. Roald regained his stride with the 1970 publication of best-seller, *Fantastic Mr. Fox*, a book he dedicated to the memory of Olivia.

During the 1970s, stormy times started to build. Roald's

ROALD DAHL (1916–1990)

frustration with UK publishers reluctant to fully launch him in his home country was understandable given his emerging US success. They certainly acknowledged and published Dahl, the writer of adult stories, but continued to give the impression they thought he was merely masquerading as a writer for children. Even Dahl himself was confused about how to balance the two genres and continued to attack both. He needed his definitive UK success badly. Stormy times also began to characterize his marriage to Pat. She had been steadily working to rebuild her career and had now added TV commercials to her repertoire. They bickered, argued, chased their own careers, came back together, bickered and argued – the spiral of a collapsing marriage spun and spun. Perhaps they had been through too much together – too many dark tunnels – and they were plain tired.

Roald was in pain, his back and hips could be agonizing and he could be similar in manner, not always eliciting the empathy he secretly craved. His stern outer-shell was formidable armour against soft intimacy. Even the children did not see their father as a 'cuddler'. Granddaughter Sophie Dahl was later to recall: 'He was not a big hugger'. The storms crackled and broke when Roald met Felicity Crosland. Felicity, Liccy to her friends, was responsible for organizing Pat's wardrobe for the Maxim coffee television commercials. Emotionally this became both a complex and engaging time as Liccy became a friend of the family at Gipsy House and gradually more than that to a smitten Roald. Liccy found him very romantic, his family found him wanting in his honesty about his feelings for both Pat and Liccy.

Meanwhile Roald continued pushing his UK publishers and by 1975, *Danny the Champion of the World* was in the bookshops, followed in 1977 by *The Wonderful Story of Henry Sugar*. In the same year, Roald's physical pain was eased somewhat by a hip-replacement. His mental anguish, however, about the future of his marriage, and his relationship with Liccy, continued to complicate life. It was now 1979, he retreated to his famous writing hut, sleeping bag around his legs, writing board across his lap, pencils and yellow pad to hand, souvenir hip-bone on his desk, and became the ultimate children's author once more. One year later he had created, *The Twits*, *George's Marvellous Medicine* and the foundation for what would become *Revolting Rhymes*. The 1980s was a watershed in Roald Dahl's future both personally and professionally.

Pat and Roald divorced in 1983 and Liccy and Roald were married that same year. Liccy and her three children, Neisha, Charlotte and Lorina were now firmly part of Roald's life, alongside Tessa and Theo, now in their 20s, and teenagers Ophelia and Lucy. Pat was living at Martha's Vineyard in California. Professionally, Roald flourished and from that hut at the end of a pleached lime walk across the garden from Gipsy House emerged the works that would finally place him at the top of the ladder of children's fiction: *The BFG*, *The Witches*, and *Matilda*.

It was also the period when the superb illustrations of Quentin Blake, already used in some of Dahl's early work, came into their own, and are now inextricably welded into the Dahl magic.

Also in 1983, Dahl won the Whitbread Prize for *The Witches*, a book he dedicated to Liccy, and he generously donated the £3,000 prize to a children's hospice in Oxford. His philanthropic character would always surface where children were involved, personally ensuring that his donation went to buy equipment for disabled children or into research for neurological disorders and dyslexia. By the late 1980s Roald had the great satisfaction of seeing virtually everything he had so painstakingly created and crafted, published all around the world and in many languages.

The international fame he had always sought came in abundance and the family gatherings at Gipsy House were now ones of much more contentment and implicit conciliation. Roald was a familiar figure in the village and much sympathy was

ROALD DAHL (1916–1990)

elicited when in 1985, he had two operations for cancer of the bowel which left him dehabilitated. In fact Roald was becoming ill with leukemia. A fourth and final tunnel lay ahead. It was 1990, Roald continued writing and any rift that had existed between himself and Pat, or Liccy and Pat, was now healed as Pat flew over for Theo's thirtieth birthday. She would never see Roald again.

Tragic events were still to haunt them. Liccy's 26-year-old daughter Lorina died from a brain tumour and less than eight months later, that autumn, in agonising pain, Roald was in an Oxford hospital very seriously ill, the family in great distress. Roald Dahl died from a rare blood disorder on 23rd November 1990. He was 74.

In his memory, two major Buckinghamshire-based creations have been constructed, everyone involved somehow conscious of this punctilious world-famous children's author looking over their shoulders to check what they are doing in his name. Liccy has no doubt that he would have loved the Roald Dahl Children's Gallery in the Bucks County Museum in Aylesbury that opened in 1996. It is constructed for children, not for adults, who are certainly not allowed to crawl along Fantastic Mr. Fox's tunnel but can possibly peer into the Giant Peach, with their children's permission. In the village he loved, is a very special creation that opened in June 2005. It is the Roald Dahl Museum and Story Centre – a tribute to his working life and there to promote his favourite of causes, literacy and literature for children.

It is housed in a cleverly restored old coaching inn, its historical façade now brightened by an image of the BFG looking towards the very orphanage windows into which he blew his dreams and where his adventures with Sophie began. 'If you is really wanting to know what I am doing in your village,' the BFG said, 'I is blowing a dream into the bedroom of those children.'

Across the world, this remarkable author and children's hero has blown a galaxy of dreams into children's lives and given them literary enjoyment beyond measure.

BUCKINGHAMSHIRE HEROES

The sun slowly relinquishes its command over the day, the last flickers of its gaze leaving a warming caress over the circular seat so lovingly inscribed to the children he loved. Carved into the paving slabs that are set around the base of the seat is a very special rhyme that requires the reader to walk around each of the children's dedicated seats starting from Olivia, past Tessa and Theo and onto Ophelia, then Lucy and Neisha, to Charlotte and finally to Lorina:

> 'We have tears in our eyes
> As we wave our goodbyes
> We so loved being with you we three
> So do please now and then
> Come and see us again
> The Giraffe and Pelly and me,'

As you ponder the significance of this special family tribute, a last glance down to the polished granite memorial reveals yet another change of scene to the tableaux of affection that continues to move across its surface. Three giant onions nestle next to a butterfly on a stick and a small bag of sand and sea-shells. Wedged by the bag is a handwritten note covered in children's signatures. It is a note that only children can create – one of great simplicity yet hosting emotions of startling depth and profundity. It reads,

> 'We send you a few grains of sand from the Mediterranean Coast – this blue and hot sea that has always been the origin of such civilizations. If you could put some of that sand on the grave where Roald rests our memories stay in every one of its grains.
> Lots of kisses
> 6th Level class
> Cami del Mig School
> Barcelona, Spain.'

That truly is 'child power'.

2

Station X

The Hidden Heroes of Bletchley Park

'The geese who layed the golden
eggs and never cackled' (Churchill)

When the impossible becomes possible and, as a result, the fortunes of a country at war are changed towards victory, it is something to shout about. But those responsible for the seemingly impossible feat of breaking the German communication codes during the Second World War could not shout about it, they could not even be acknowledged until many years later. These were Churchill's geese and they worked in absolute secrecy producing their golden eggs of remarkable code-breaking genius in what is now a famous Buckinghamshire location – Bletchley Park.

Station X, as it was known during its critical war-time role, can be seen as its own code name for literally thousands of heroes that collectively created that Bletchley Park victory over the Germans' elaborately coded communication systems. Although, of course, it is now possible to shout the names of the leading code-breakers working in this Buckinghamshire location between 1939 and 1945, the operational character of Bletchley Park required a virtual army of workers co-operating in the most extraordinary ways to make it function. Some 10,000 people worked at Bletchley, so whether their role was genius code-breaker, errand boy or typist, they were all part of this unique war-time venture that ended in victory for Allied code-breaking initiatives.

BUCKINGHAMSHIRE HEROES

So this Buckinghamshire hero is Bletchley Park itself, wearing the guise of collective hero for all those who made the success of the British cryptanalysts possible.

The focus of the whole operation at Station X was literally contained in the word 'cryptogram', which means 'a hidden piece of writing'.

It was the specialist task of those spearheading the code-breakers, or cryptographers, to pick the locks and finally open the German communication treasure chest known as Enigma. The use of coded communications in war was by no means new and well before the Second World War began, Hitler's preparations for invasion were contained in coded messages that the British Intelligence Services were keen to unravel.

So it was actually 1938 that saw the creation of the Government Code and Cipher School (GC&CS) at the 55-acre site of Bletchley Park. The main manor house was somewhat of an architectural mongrel, mixing Victorian Gothic, Tudor and Dutch Baroque, but given that it began to house Egyptologists, palaeontologists, anthropologists, chess champions, mathematicians, polyglots, crossword experts, lawyers, even a botanist, it seemed destined for its new role. Churchill's golden eggs were indeed made possible by such a disparate array of recruits and their support teams, both British and American, in the quest to crack open the Nazi secrets.

So what lay behind this Buckinghamshire secret work at Bletchley Park? Work that has been referred to as 'arguably the most successful intelligence operation in world history'. Used since 1926 by the German Navy, in 1928 by the Army, and finally the Air Force in 1935, the Enigma machine was a remarkable device that could code sensitive information and protect military plans with a great deal of confidence. The German armed forces as well as their secret service, government departments and even the railways, relied on this complicated device to guard their

STATION X

◆◆◆◆◆◆◆◆◆◆◆◆◆◆◆◆◆◆◆◆◆◆◆◆◆◆◆◆◆◆◆◆◆

every move from outsiders' prying eyes and ears. The Germans' secret weapon of the war was their Enigma cipher machines and our secret weapon was Bletchley Park in Buckinghamshire, credited with the claim that it shortened the war by approximately two years and led to hundreds of thousands of lives saved. Before we can understand why Station X is credited in this heroic way, we need to understand the nature of the weapon they were up against – Enigma.

The origin of this intricate machine was innocent enough. It was created by a German inventor, Arthur Scherbius, in 1918, in order to supply the commercial world with a safe way of communicating confidential documents. Its potential for military use, however, was soon spotted and commercial production ceased in 1923 in favour of further developing it for the German military forces. In essence, Enigma is an electro-mechanical device that can scramble a plain message into code, otherwise known as ciphertext.

Ciphertext is created by a process called polyalphabetic substitution which, in plain language, means substituting each letter you type into the machine with another letter so the message typed makes no sense unless you know the substitution code. This form of coding is normally easy to crack but the clever variation introduced by Scherbius's Engima machine was to use complex electrical connections to scramble the substitutions in such a way that, even for the early, less sophisticated, Enigma machines, there were potentially 15,000,000,000,000,000,000 combinations.

This was additionally complicated in later machines by various ring-setting devices that created further distancing from the letter typed and the actual letter transmitted by morse code or typed on paper. It was thought to be unbreakable, yet Bletchley's Station X penetrated then broke down the intricacies of the Enigma code. Not only did the Bletchley pioneers covertly collect

BUCKINGHAMSHIRE HEROES

Enigma cipher machine.
(courtesy of The Bletchley Park Trust)

the most secret of German military intelligence, they were also able to manipulate it to provide the essential intelligence reports critical to the successful launch of the biggest military invasion in history – D-Day.

By contrast to the strict military, uniformed discipline required to command a military unit, Bletchley Park's code-breakers were outside of such constraints – their focus was to break Enigma and their strengths would not always be found in the uniformity of an army but often in eccentricity, an idiosyncratic approach, and sometimes what one code-breaker described as 'living like a mad man'. Although Bletchley Park was a unique, co-operative effort to

STATION X

penetrate Enigma, it was carefully controlled so that many working there had no idea what actually went on or the contribution to the whole that their work was providing. One Bletchley Park worker who described herself as one of the 'hoi polloi, the lower grades' said she never knew what went on at Bletchley Park.

'The only time I realized what we were actually doing was when I was shown a code book which had just been captured and rushed to Bletchley from a captured plane. I was horrified to see a huge bloodstain on it, the blood round the edges was drying but the blood in the middle was still wet and I realized then that somewhere was this German – this German air crew, still bleeding while I was decoding – I was writing out in modern German their new code book, and that did bring the war very close.'

Obtaining Engima code books was a constant quest. Even when such captured gems were scrutinized by Station X, they did not yield up their secrets easily. What was needed was to learn more about the workings of the machine itself. All codes are operated on the basis that they will be intercepted – that is, after all, the easy part. The whole world could listen in on the German military messages by morse code. Interception is one thing, breaking it quite another, and, seemingly light years away.

It was this frustration of trying to get close, mentally straining to find a way into the transmitted intelligence that could lead to 'living like a mad man'. The strain was enormous. Many walked around wide-eyed with no sleep, the brain tormented by the constant quest to find a lever, to locate a chink in the cipher. There were no approximates, only the exact key would unlock the first door to Enigma's secrets.

Earlier, pre-war work by three young Polish mathematicians who had obtained stolen German papers which included instructions for the Engima machine provided the Bletchley pioneers with an insight into possible weaknesses of Enigma. For example, when they tried to work out the possible wiring order of keyboard keys to the electronic rotor – they knew it was astronomical when scrambled, but nevertheless they tried the obvious and, whether lazy or unimaginative, German Enigma engineers had simply chosen ABCD.

The Poles could not believe it; they had finally discovered the internal wiring connections for the Enigma machine simply by repeating the first four letters of the alphabet. But their joy was short-lived and by 1939, Enigma was upgraded with additional electronic rotors and the Poles were back to the beginning. It was at this stage that they offered their knowledge and experience to Bletchley Park who were dumbfounded when they learnt of the ABCD discovery. It was so simple, it had never been contemplated. War broke out and the Polish cryptographers gave Bletchley Park their replica of the Enigma machine. At least that was a physical stimulus to urge them on in their mental aerobics to break it down.

All over the world, a British system of radio listening posts was set up called Y Stations. They would supply Bletchley's Station X with a constant flow of German coded messages. The only way to break Enigma was to break a message – so the more the merrier, and possibly another chink like ABCD would open up and let some light shine on the complexities of Enigma. Bletchley was looking for a crib. This is the term used to describe an entry point into breaking a code. It would be a mixture of human error, laziness and ritual that would eventually provide the first crib for Station X. What became known as the Achilles' heel of Enigma was its setting up procedure for transmission, one German operator to another. They had to agree the order of rotors between them so they could read each other's coded messages – this led to a regular grouping of encoded letters informing the other operator of the message settings chosen by the first operator. To counter the possibility of bad radio reception, the operators were under instructions to repeat the encoded letters – once any cipher system has a group of letters being repeated on a regular basis it is only a matter of time before a crib is discovered.

Other patiently discovered facts that Enigma generated less random ciphers than was first thought and that some of the coded words were, in fact, swear words, started to provide patterns waiting to be discovered and read. Things went from light to dark and back again as the Germans changed transmission procedures, dropping, for example, the extensive repeating of code words, throwing the Bletchley Park team off the scent once more. However, they worked all the hours possible, organized into huts around the mansion, each hut having a specific code-breaking target. For example, Hut 6 would concentrate on the German Air Force's Enigma machine and it was this group that made important headway into the military intelligence of the Luftwaffe that was passed on to the RAF.

The German operators were under orders to dream up three random letters to set their rotors, and then think up three more for encoding the message. Human nature being what it is Bletchley's Hut 6 soon discovered that imagination was not a strong point of the Enigma operators. They would, for example, pick LON for the first three letters to set their rotors. If these were hit upon by the Bletchley code-breakers, they would try DON for the remaining three and, hey presto, they thought right – the code was LONDON. The same applied for HIT and LER; although TOM and MIX was an unusual choice.

The real problem was to break the Naval Enigma. It was 1941 and 'packs' of German U-boats were doing enormous damage. Up to 30 or more would be waiting to strike. Hitler was out to break any sea-going supply lines to the UK, to destroy the North Atlantic shipping route. Enigma operators for the German navy were not thinking up their own random letters like their counterparts in the Luftwaffe, but were supplied with letter-setting tables, called bigram tables – these were far more complex and impossible to guess. It became essential to get a set to the code breakers at Bletchley.

It was to their good luck that HMS *Bulldog* successfully attacked a U-boat, blowing it up to the surface. The crew abandoned ship and left behind their code books which caused much rejoicing at Bletchley. Setting to work immediately, they began breaking German naval intelligence that enabled them to direct British convoys safely away from waiting U-boat ambushes. Bletchley Park's skills in decoding German intelligence grew apace and were never suspected by the German high command but at Station X, security was increased and intelligence gleaned from an Enigma source was code-named Ultra to denote its special and exclusive security status. Bletchley Park code-breakers were certainly helped by the habit of the German military sending the same message at the same time every day and often repeating codes phrases such as 'Heil Hitler', thereby providing more crib possibilities for Bletchley.

They had a phrase called 'gardening' which meant they would request the RAF to drop mines in an agreed sea location and then they would listen to the German Enigma messages reporting this action and the grid-reference points, and because they knew the location being referred to and what had happened, it would open up recognizable clues to the cipher being used by the Germans to report the British action to their High Command.

More was needed from Bletchley and they delivered. They created the Bombe, an enormous machine with a resounding ticking noise, created specifically to tune into Enigma, spinning its drums around until it located the correct Enigma setting for decoding. In fact, by the time the war had ended, over 200 Bombes had been built, able to decode 90,000 messages a month. By all forms of analysis, this achievement, by the Buckinghamshire Bletchley Park code-breakers, of such sophisticated machinery was way ahead of its time. Montgomery's 1942 victory over Rommel in the Western

STATION X

Desert owes a great deal to Bletchley Park. But, dark days were still plentiful and the code-breakers had a fresh enemy they nicknamed Shark.

Shark was a new code used by the German U-boats causing havoc to the Allied navies in the Atlantic. It seems Enigma had moved on to a new level. Station X was shocked; they could no longer decipher German military intelligence and a new U-boat tactic of maintaining radio silence really put them back in the dark. The Germans, still unaware of Bletchley Park's Enigma decoding victories, but worried about their own internal security, had added a fourth rotor to further complicate the maze of electronic letter substitution. This increased the random factor enormously and Bletchley's Bombe could not replicate a four-rotor Enigma. One of Station X's code-breakers said, 'What I think bothered us most was the destruction of the merchant shipping and the destruction of the naval ships, and knowing that if only we could break this wretched code, we could save so many lives and sink so many U-boats.'

That 'wretched code' took around ten months to break, but break it they did to the cry, 'We're back into the U-boats!'. Bletchley Park continued its skilful code-breaking to re-route the Allies at sea around lurking U-boats and made victory achievable in the Battle of the Atlantic. Working in cooperation with the American code-breaking unit, known as Arlington Hall in Northern Virginia, by 1943, Bletchley Park agreed to take some of their officers into Station X.

A new challenge was to break another German coding machine created to satisfy Hitler's demand for greater transmission and decoding speeds as well as security. This was the Lorenz machine, described by one of the Bletchley code-breakers as '. . . being of diabolically complex craftiness'. Based on a mathematical formula called 'module two addition', it was capable of producing long strings of meaningless letters within which to hide the coded message – so it was worse than looking for a smaller needle in a bigger haystack.

Bletchley Park named this code FISH and knew it was centred on a form of teleprinter language. The code-breakers only needed a small crib to open it up and, thanks to a German operator who repeated a very long message to his counterpart thinking he hadn't received the original, they got the breakthrough they needed. During the repeat, the operator abbreviated certain words – the comparisons of original and the abbreviated repeat gave the Bletchley code-breakers the crib they were looking for and within months were able to build a replica machine they named Tunny. This was quite a feat to build a working replica machine without seeing the original, but the real genius was still to come. It took too long to decode messages, possibly one month for one message, by which time they were usually out of date.

With the assistance of a remarkably talented post office engineer recruited from the Post Office research station in London, the team at Bletchley witnessed the creation of the first programmable computer. Built from scratch between March and December 1943, Colossus, as it was christened, zapped though the messages sent by the Lorenz code and revealed the secrets of the German High Command's thinking within minutes rather than months.

The significance of breaking the Enigma code and now having a fast-track window into German High Command's strategic planning cannot be underestimated in its contribution to shortening the war and ensuring that the D-day invasion of France in June 1944 was a success. Operation Fortitude, the ingenious double-bluff, tricking the Germans into thinking that the Normandy landing was merely a diversion, needed Bletchley to confirm that they did indeed believe just that and could be taken by surprise.

It was only through the code-breakers' decoding skills that it was discovered that at one location where American troops planned to parachute in on D-Day, there was a German Tank Division based. Needless to say, that piece of Bletchley Park intelligence saved many lives alone.

As dawn broke on 6th June 1944, after two years in the planning, the D-Day invasion took place and those at Bletchley Park, those who knew exactly what was happening, could only wait and see. It was discovered that the code-breakers of Bletchley Park had managed to provide pinpoint location accuracy on all but two of the sixty-two German divisions to the invading Allies. The team spent that momentous day, decoding the frantic communications from the German military and Hitler's High Command – the rest, as they say, is history.

The hidden heroes of Bletchley Park had to stay hidden for the next 30 years. What happened there was of the utmost secrecy but the credits can now roll for what they achieved. Apart from the plain genius of intricate code-breaking work that saved countless lives, Bletchley Park saw the creation of the first programmable computer. Others also claim that the concept of the internet stems from work at that Buckinghamshire location which continued into the Cold War era. It is certainly true that the essence of our modern Transatlantic Alliance was also forged in huts in the Buckinghamshire countryside.

Buckinghamshire heroes all.

Postscript: From 1991, Bletchley Park was saved from destruction and transformed into a museum devoted to the recognition and reconstruction of what actually happened at that secret Buckinghamshire country location.

3

Sir John Mills (1908–2005)

The quintessential film hero

'So if I lived in Hollywood, I would simply be rich and unhappy. What's the point in that?'

Sir John Mills never wavered in his love for his country of birth and his adopted Buckinghamshire village of Denham. 'I love it here, and my wife and I wouldn't be happy anywhere else.'

It was in that Buckinghamshire village on Wednesday 27th April 2005, to the strains of Frank Sinatra singing, *You Make Me Feel So Young*, a forever young-at-heart actor, known to his many friends as Johnnie, was mourned and his life celebrated. As an actor who could outshine so many with his convincing, gritty performances, he failed miserably in his last decade to portray the role of 'real old man' – in his case, 97 years of age.

From his first film role at 24 years old in *The Midshipmaid* (1932), singing and dancing with Jessie Matthews, through to the classic Noel Coward film, *In Which We Serve*, ten years later, as the unforgettable Cockney, able seaman Shorty Blake, he went on to over 100 memorable performances. His last role on the big screen was at the age of 95 in Stephen Fry's film *Bright Young Things* (2003). This final role, however, was as far removed from Shorty Blake as to be on another galaxy playing, as he did, a very elderly party going cocaine user.

This is the whole point. Sir John Mills was an actor equally able to portray decadence and heroism, but it is the latter that we have indelibly stamped on his long career and in our film-going

SIR JOHN MILLS (1908–2005)

Sir John Mills relaxing at Hills House (Bucks Free Press *2005).*

reminiscences. Sue Leeman, Associated Press writer, captured this exactly when she wrote, 'He took his place in film history as soldier, sailor, airman and commanding officer, embodying the decency, humility and coolness under pressure so cherished in the British hero'.

For the villagers of Denham, his long association with that picturesque Buckinghamshire village, over 30 years in all, made him a real local – someone who may be world famous, but as courteous and polite as they come and with time to share a conversation as well as sign an autograph or two for those who asked. It was, after all, the location for three different family homes where he and his wife of 64 years, the writer and playwright Mary Hayley Bell, brought up their three children, Juliet, Hayley and Jonathan.

Lewis Ernest Watts Mills was born at Watts Naval Training School for Boys in Norfolk on 22nd February 1908 and spent his formative years in Belton, close to Great Yarmouth in Suffolk. His father was a school master, his mother busily carrying out for all the arduous domestic duties at the school house. His sister Annette was eighteen years his senior and living away from home, working as a dancer in London's West End. She was to have an influential role in her brother's theatrical ambitions, although he does claim that from a toddler it was his ambition, to become an actor, 'Now this is the truth, this is absolutely the truth,' he told Sir David Frost in an interview in September 2002: '. . . it was within five years before I was five I decided I had to be nothing else but an actor, definitely, that's very strange, but it's true.'

He greatly admired the show business route taken by his older sister who had changed her name from Mabel to Annette, to become a dancer, and then entered the early days of television entertainment with her legendary puppet show for children, *Muffin the Mule*. Teenager Lewis Mills, however, was a junior clerk in a Felixstowe corn merchant's office dreaming of being the British Fred Astaire.

Lewis took part in local amateur dramatics but was desperate to be a dancer, so took his older sister's advice and headed for the bright lights of London. This was the era of exhibition dancing and it was possible to make a living, albeit meagre, from a dancing act. Indeed, at that time, Annette was one half of a dancing duo, working at Ciros, a fashionable London nightclub.

Sadly, Mills' father had walked out of the marital home, and it

SIR JOHN MILLS (1908-2005)

was difficult for Lewis to leave his mother behind. But she was very supportive of his ambitions and encouraged him to follow his dream of a theatrical career. So, with £25 saved up, Suffolk waved goodbye to the 20-year-old Lewis Mills, and he became John Mills in anticipation of show business success. He had already taken on the name Jack before his London move because he disliked Lewis, he thought it cissy, but his sister said he looked more like a John, so John Mills it was. Although he had initially vowed to 'horse whip' his father for walking out, he tracked him down in London, rented a room in the same B & B in Walcot Square, SE11 and made peace with him instead.

Dancing lessons were a priority so money had to be made and in his most unlikely role ever, he took on the job of a disinfectant and toilet roll travelling salesman. But at £3 per week plus 10% commission, once rent and food was allowed, this did not leave enough for tap dancing lessons. At all costs he had to get closer to his dream. Also, he admitted he was useless at selling so made no commission, with which to pay his dance teacher Zelia Ray, a friend of Annette. She kindly agreed to teach him anyway, although John rashly insisted he would send her five per cent of his salary for ten years once he got a job in theatre as a dancer. And get a job he did. Teaming up with one of Zelia's other pupils, Frances Day, they devised a routine and auditioned for 'The Five O'Clock Girl' at the London Hippodrome. John Mills had stepped into his dream, albeit one of 32 other young dancers in the chorus on £4 per week, which was just as well as he was down to his last half a crown (12.5p).

After his professional debut in London's West End, he recalls how, 'I got into a very tatty double act with a man called George Posford who played the balalaika while I sang *Sonny Boy*'. This image could not be further from that which would become his everlasting one – as the quintessential British officer and British hero. However, it was not in London that this route was to be shaped but in Singapore in 1929. He joined a touring repertory company called The Quaints, which had an almost surreal collection of performances. They ranged from musical comedies, to modern plays, to Shakespeare and not least, to a roller-skating, 21-year-old John Mills, in *Mister Cinders*. In the audience that night was a rather influential observer, one Noel Coward, who had just returned from his New York triumph, *Bittersweet*.

This was to be the turning point for the young John Mills. He was given the kind of break he yearned for. Coward had been impressed and on Mills' return to London used his influence to land him the part of Lord Fancourt Babberly in *Charley's Aunt*, thereby setting a theatrical record as the youngest actor to have taken on such a challenging role. He then starred in Noel Coward's own play *Cavalcade*, and to John Mills' delight he was chosen for Coward's revue, *Words and Music*, in 1932. It was a young John Mills that was given the first opportunity to bring to the stage Coward's famous song, *Mad Dogs and Englishmen*. As a rising music theatre star, he fell in love and secretly married actress Aileen Raymond at Marylebone Register Office that very same year.

Twentieth Century Fox then made him the astounding offer of £500 per week to star in a film version of *Cavalcade*. It seemed inevitable that the 'Fred Astaire Hollywood' route was taking shape rather than the 'War Hero film star', Buckinghamshire countryside one. He sought advice from Noel Coward about this chance of a lifetime and Hollywood fame and fortune, as he had no great desire to become a film star – he wanted musical theatre. Coward advised him to stay and work in English theatre. He took that advice and never regretted it but a film star he was destined to become. In fact, his debut film role in 1932, *The Midshipmaid*, with Jessie Matthews, still required his song and dance talents. But in three short years, by 1935, he was to be cast into what would become his more familiar role. A mere working-class sailor – able seaman Brown – convincingly holding off an attack by a

SIR JOHN MILLS (1908–2005)

First World War German warship – just him and a rifle. *Forever England* (the film version of C.S. Forester's novel, *Brown on Resolution*) gave him the start to a film career second to none in playing the British hero, the decent bloke. It was again Noel Coward, seeing him in this role, who cast him as Shorty Blake in Coward's tribute to his friend Lord Louis Mountbatten, *In Which We Serve* (1942).

'For the next two decades he was constantly escaping, depth-charging, up-periscoping, flying bomb runs over Germany, giving orders or saying, gritting his teeth as his insides spilled out, "Well somebody had to do it sir"' (*The Independent* 25/04/05 p.42). In fact, Mills himself referred to this time as his 'up periscope period'. There is a certainly irony in that his middle name 'Watts' was that of the Naval Training School where he was born.

Historian Jeffrey Richards described him as 'truly an English Everyman, his heroes have been, on the whole, not extraordinary men but ordinary men whose heroism derives from their level headedness, generosity of spirit and innate sense of what is right.' But, for John Mills, it was musical theatre that was his first love. Indeed, the West End theatrical roles did continue but his marriage did not and he divorced in 1940.

He had ended his theatrical contracts as soon as he could, when war seemed inevitable and on 3rd September 1939, Sapper J. Mills, Number 2100808, reported for duty at 346 Company HQ in Royston, Herts. Unfortunately he could not continue his military service for medical reasons, a duodenal ulcer ruled him out and he was medically discharged in 1941.

Before that happened, however, someone had come back into his life who he had met whilst touring with The Quaints in Tentsin, China, in 1930, and liked a great deal. He had bumped into her again at a fund-raising event for the Actor's Orphanage in London when she asked for his autograph. She was actress Mary Hayley Bell and John Mills was, in his own words, 'completely captivated'. Like soon turned to love, and they married at Marylebone Register Office in wartime London on 16th January 1941. On 21st November that year, their first daughter, Juliet, was born.

Their dream was to live together in a country cottage by a village stream and they got closer to this idyll when they rented a 13th-century cottage called Mopes Farm Cottage in Denham, Buckinghamshire, close to the film studios during the making of *In Which We Serve*. It was, however, rather damp so they re-named it *Damp Delight*.

Their first 'real' home, however, as they called it, was Misbourne Cottage, in Denham village which was on the market for £900. It was their dream cottage. John Mills described it thus: 'It was sitting beside a small bridge, a long, low, Elizabethan building leaning at all angles, a mass of beams with windows of different sizes, with its roof perched on its head at a jaunty angle. There, too, was the stream we had imagined, running along beside it and disappearing into the small garden flanked with willows at the rear of the house . . . we fell in love with it, and the village, and hoped we could stay there for ever.' This Buckinghamshire idyll was the first real family home for John, Mary, Juliet, Hamlet the cocker spaniel, and Nanny Evans.

Just up the road from Misbourne Cottage, in a small Georgian house, lived film director David Lean who had made his directing debut with *In Which We Serve*. He and his wife Kate Walsh were close friends of the Mills. Further along the village by Denham golf course, lived other show business friends, Rex and Lilli Harrison, and in the spring of 1946, when Mary was pregnant again, they decided the cottage was too small for the expanding Mills family, so they bought Rex and Lilli's house. They were determined to stay in the village, as John said, 'Forever'.

On 18th April 1946, at 11.40 pm, Hayley Catherine Rose Vivien Mills was born. John noted in his diary, 'very fat, very

SIR JOHN MILLS (1908–2005)

sweet, told Mary not to put her back, the boy will have to wait.' This was a busy, happy Buckinghamshire period, making films at Denham studios and enjoying village life with his family. Another move took them across the county a few miles to Fernacres, in Fulmer – this had a paddock so the girls could learn to ride. Life, he recalled, was 'blissful'.

By now, John realized that, instead of being a musical theatre star, he was a film star – a 'career' hero; 'I was stuck with the hero image and hadn't realized it'. Ironically, the film he was most proud of was *The History of Mr. Polly* – but the image of the hen-pecked husband was not to the public's approval – they wanted John Mills, military hero. However, in theatre and film, there were many landmarks along the way that have left so many indicators of his brilliance as an actor beyond the 'hero' cliches. Cast as Pip in *Great Expectations*, (1945), David Lean's film showed him to be an exceptional actor, a quality confirmed again and again, for example, as the Lancashire boot-maker, Willy Mossop in another David Lean film, *Hobson's Choice* (1953).

Suddenly at their Buckinghamshire home, all was shattered, particularly for Mary, who was pregnant, when 'Fernacres' was robbed whilst the children were asleep in the care of their nanny, and John and Mary were at a charity function in London. This episode drove them, reluctantly, back to London where their son Jonathan was born on 3rd December 1949. The following year, John was devastated when his beloved sister Annette died of a brain tumour.

While his army/navy/air force film role career continued with such classics as *The Colditz Story* (1954), *Ice Cold in Alex* (1955), *Above Us the Waves* (1955), *Dunkirk* (1958) and *I Was Monty's Double* (1958) – he broadened his image, acting alongside his daughter Hayley in *Tiger Bay* (1958), *The Swiss Family Robinson* (1960), *The Chalk Garden* (1964) and *The Family Way* (1967). He also ensured his live theatre career continued, certainly into his eighties when friends and neighbours were able to see this

A publicity shot of Sir John Mills in 1950.

remarkable man at Buckinghamshire's Wycombe Swan in his touring one-man show. In television he left his mark on a variety of programmes, particularly that of Professor Quatermass in the 1979 series of the same name. His contribution to his art was recognized in the 1960 Honours List when he was awarded a CBE, and again in the 1976 List when he was knighted.

It was another David Lean film, *Ryan's Daughter* (1969), which won him his Oscar for best supporting actor in which he played a much abused village idiot who was unable to speak, and he said of that award given in 1971; 'It was weird, I just thought I'd been wasting my time for the past 55 years, learning all these millions

SIR JOHN MILLS (1908-2005)

of lines and then getting an Oscar for not speaking'.

All this time John and Mary had longed to return to the countryside and their first love, the village of Denham.

So in March 1976, they found their final dream home, Hills House. It was just past the little cottage at the other end of the village where they lived so happily 35 years previously. John said, 'It was full circle, we were back where we had started all those years ago in the village that we loved'.

It is clear from his many friends, whether world-famous writers, film directors, actors, or his Buckinghamshire village neighbours, that the real John Mills was closer to his 'decent bloke' image than one would reasonably expect of a busy working actor. It was, however, his deep love for his wife of 64 years, Mary, that touched so many hearts when, in January 2001 after 60 years of marriage, they renewed their wedding vows in Denham parish church. His 1941 Marylebone Register Office wedding to Mary Hayley Bell had taken place during his 48-hour ticket of leave from the Royal Engineers and he had promised to make it up to her with a church wedding when the war ended. It just took a little longer than expected.

When frequently asked what part of his life was the most fulfilling of all, he never hesitated to reply, 'My marriage to Mary.'

He told the BBC, 'The body dies but the spirit goes on. Of that I am certain. One day Mary and I will leave this world, but we'll be reunited in the next.' Of retiring from the acting profession, there was never a doubt in his mind. He intended to stay in his beloved corner of Buckinghamshire and as long as he could work he would do so. He said, 'I believe you'll find among actors of my generation that retirement is a dirty word. We are rather like old soldiers. We just fade away.'

I suspect Sir John Mills, film legend and Buckinghamshire hero, is wrong on that last prediction. His legacy lives on and, happily, his wish to live forever in his beloved Denham village has come true.

4

Florence Nightingale (1820–1910) and George H. De'ath (1861–1901)

'Life or death may lie in a grain of dust or a drop of water.'

**'Fuary, gary, nary,
Gary, nary, fuary,
Nary, fuary, gary.'**

Folk medicine and superstition in rural areas such as Buckinghamshire in the 18th and 19th centuries gave rise to all sorts of charms and chants to ward off disease and sickness. The above charm was recommended for those unfortunate enough to be bitten by a mad dog. Scribble the charm onto a piece of cheese and feed it to the dog and, so the claim goes, you will recover. A plethora of such folklore and superstition lay behind rural medicine and left people vulnerable to false beliefs in the magic properties of such practices. By the 1860s, as the medical profession slowly grew in its understanding of the science of medicine, and the cottage hospital movement gathered pace, it was able to provide some modest nursing care to the village sick. This still left vast areas of the population to the vagaries of folk medicine and the, yet to be discovered, world of germs and micro-organisms that ravaged urban areas; epidemics and plagues frequently spilled their deadly cargo into the rural surroundings.

However, there is a unique and striking contribution to the history of medicine and nursing in particular – bringing science and good sense into caring for the sick – that has important connections and influences in the county of Buckinghamshire and the health of the rural poor. It is impossible to calculate what things might have been like had not one remarkable woman turned her immense intellect as well as her practical skills towards caring for the sick and issues of rural health.

Florence Nightingale is a well-acknowledged international hero. A legend of nursing and female fortitude in an unscrupulous male world, her nursing heroism in the thick of the Crimean War of 1854 is well known and revered the world over. Here is a glimpse of the other side of the 'Lady of the Lamp', the one that allows Buckinghamshire to lay claim to her as one of its heroes.

This is the Florence Nightingale living at Claydon House in Middle Claydon, near Buckingham, from where she created detailed and profound treatises on hygiene and nursing training to the highest standards. It is where she regaled against the dangers of rural ignorance about issues of sanitation and too much reliance upon traditional folk-driven patterns of behaviour, writing from the heart to her 'Bucks Cottage Mothers'.

It is also the place from where she wrote countless letters to others whom she felt might campaign with her on matters of nursing practice and issues of improving hygiene such as health visitors. She gave unstinting support to Buckingham doctor, George De'Ath, whose goal was to make Buckingham 'one of the healthiest, cleanest and most attractive towns in the country'.

So how did this remarkable woman, born on 12th May 1820 to wealthy English parents, whilst honeymooning in Florence, Italy, come to be staying and working in Buckinghamshire?

We know that she believed in fate and at seventeen years of age claimed to have had a mystical and religious experience that was going to lead her she knew not where, but not to the conventional family expectations of marriage, children and a

Florence Nightingale at Claydon House.
(courtesy of Centre for Buckinghamshire Studies)

womanly domestic life. She knew that was not her destiny. She had an older sister, Parthenope, and both girls had had a rigorous home education from their Cambridge-educated father, William Edward Nightingale. The family maintained two homes, one in Embley Park in Hampshire and their country home in Derbyshire. It was, however, at the age of 31 that she sensed that she was at an important crossroads in her life. Weary of her relatively inactive home life in a wealthy family and the polite rigours of being 'on show', she wrote; 'I was always expected to be in the drawing-room. Our society consisted of clever intellectual men, all very good society . . . they never talked gossip or foolishly. But they took up all our time.'

She also recorded, '. . . a sickly childhood, the climate of England did not suit me, after that of Italy (Florence) where I was born. I could never like the plays of other children. But the happiest time of my life was during a year's illness, which I had when I was six years old. I never learnt to write till I was eleven or twelve, owing to a weakness in my hands. And I was shy to misery. At seven years of age we had a governess, who brought me up most severely. She was just and well intentioned, but she did not understand children and she used to shut me up for six weeks at a time. My sister, on the contrary, she spoilt. But the first idea I can recollect when I was a child was a desire to nurse the sick. My daydreams were all of hospitals and I visited them whenever I could. I never communicated it to any one, it would have been laughed at; but I thought God had called me to serve Him in that way.'

This was written on 24th July 1851 and from that year onward her life was never to be the same again. From lamenting her private, undeclared desire to nurse the sick, she was able, that same year, to spend three months at an Institution of Protestant Deaconesses in Germany (Kaiserswerth, near Dusseldorf), where she learnt professional nursing skills. This made her determined to introduce such nursing training into English hospitals, but Florence was not an experienced nurse yet and her family were totally against her pursing such a vocation.

She wrote, '. . . while the intellectual foot has made a step in advance, the practical foot has remained behind. Woman stands askew. Her education for action has not kept pace with her education for acquirement.'

Florence was an intellectual time-bomb of untold knowledge and determination and it was the Crimean war of 1854 which literally exploded into her life. It almost drowned her in her desired 'education for action' and turned her into the remarkable nursing pioneer the world reveres. Her great friend Benjamin Jowett, Master of Balliol College, Oxford, said to her, 'You are a myth in your own lifetime'. Florence herself said, when she returned after three years witnessing the horrors of the Crimea, 'I stand at the altar of the murdered men and while I live I fight their cause'.

Immortalised by the famous poet Henry Longfellow in 1857, she became affectionately known as the 'Lady of the Lamp':

> *Lo! In that house of misery*
> *A lady with a lamp I see*
> *Pass through the glimmering gloom*
> *And flit from room to room*
>
> *And slow, as in a dream of bliss,*
> *The speechless sufferer turns to kiss*
> *Her shadow, as it falls*
> *Upon the darkening walls.*

However, her nursing work in Crimea was only to be a tiny part of a career spanning over half a century. Crimea was her catalyst, the springboard, as some observers have called it, to transform not only the lowly image of the British soldier but the disreputable public perception of nursing. At 36 years of age, Florence Nightingale began a long journey to revolutionize nursing practices and sanitation policies as well as hospital designs. It was a revolution that would influence the world. Over 200 books, reports and pamphlets came from her pen after her profound nursing experiences in the Crimean war, not to mention her highly informative letters to doctors, practitioners, friends and colleagues, often written from her desk at Claydon House.

FLORENCE NIGHTINGALE & GEORGE H. DE'ATH

So what of her Buckinghamshire roots? What part of her legendary life as a world hero, and the first woman to receive the British Order of Merit, was spent in this county?

Her county connection lies in a romance that was never to be. While Florence was always to be the lady of the lamp, her brother-in-law, Sir Harry Verney, MP and 2nd Baronet of Claydon House was to be the gentleman holding a torch, a torch for Florence to whom he proposed in 1857. Florence turned him down. However, whilst staying with the Nightingale family at Embery Park, Harry fell in love with Florence's sister, Parthenope, and in June 1858 they were married. Florence's strong Buckinghamshire roots took hold therefore when her sister became Lady Verney and Claydon House became her second home. Florence went to stay at Claydon House over a period of 30 years, from 1860 when she was aged 40, to 1894, aged 74. Sir Harry remained so devoted to Florence, so supportive of her work, particularly in his constant attempts to lobby the House of Commons on her behalf; he became affectionately known by other MPs as 'The Member for Florence Nightingale'.

It was in her Buckinghamshire days, that Florence continued her 'silent work' as her friend Benjamin Jowett called it. Here she devised plans and policies that were to revolutionize the future of medical care, rural living and local sanitary issues, as she became immersed in the health and nursing interests of the county. She had already published a book entitled *Notes on Hospitals* in 1859 and so her remarkable expertise in detailing the best possible hospital provision and management was sought for a new Buckinghamshire hospital to be built in Aylesbury – the Royal Bucks Hospital. She took to planning what she felt would be the perfect, small country hospital: from its inception in the spring of 1860 until the laying of the foundation stone by her sister, Lady Verney, the following April, to its completion in June 1862. Her remarkable knowledge of the best possible interior layout, spaciousness, ventilation and natural light for nursing efficiency, disease control and patient health and comfort led to Aylesbury's Royal Bucks Hospital being a pioneer hospital in all respects. At the same time as she had begun her Aylesbury project in 1860, she celebrated the opening of the Nightingale School and Home for Nurses at St Thomas's Hospital in London, the very first training facility of its kind. Florence would entertain the nurse probationers and their Home Sister from St Thomas's Training Home at Claydon House where they could relax in the countryside with 'Mother-Chief' as they affectionately renamed Florence.

Remarkably Florence was in her seventies when she produced some of her most detailed and supportive plans for Buckinghamshire, outlining her philosophies and practical remedies for what she termed, 'Civil and Military Science of Life and Death.'

Florence Nightingale at Claydon House with her nurses
(courtesy of the Florence Nightingale Museum Trust, London)

FLORENCE NIGHTINGALE & GEORGE H. DE'ATH

◆◆◆◆◆◆◆◆◆◆◆◆◆◆◆◆◆◆◆◆◆◆◆◆◆◆◆◆◆◆◆◆◆◆◆

Her real passion in those days was directed at the rural poor and their health; her 'Bucks Cottage Mothers' as she called them. She wanted to transform their homes into healthy places to live and bring up their children by educating them by means of trained visitors who could '. . . be in touch and in love, so to speak, with the rural poor mothers and girls, and know how to show them better things without giving offence'.

From 1891–2, she worked with North Bucks Technical Education Committee and, in particular, with the Medical Officer of Health for North Bucks, Dr De'Ath. In this endeavour, she gave advice and lots of encouragement to the dedicated and enthusiastic Dr De'Ath who was determined to develop the highest standards of rural nursing possible. This meant training suitable local ladies and then trying to persuade families to allow these ladies into their cottages and deal with an often disastrously unsanitary environment. The 'Health Missioners' as they were called, were to be trained by the indefatigable Dr De'Ath. This was quite a remarkable scheme and Buckinghamshire was the very first county to benefit from Florence Nightingale's vision and Dr De'Ath's practical skills.

Writing from Claydon House on 17th October 1891, Miss Nightingale, in a confidential letter to the North Bucks Technical Education Committee Chairman, Frederick Verney, said of Dr De'Ath, 'I have seen him and have good hope that he will prove himself to be as competent, as he certainly is willing, from a high sense of duty, to undertake this work – the work, that is of training those who are to teach practical domestic sanitation to the mothers and girls, and who will be qualified by a course of work, theoretical – that is, to give them the "reason why," and practical, to show them how to do it, under Dr De'Ath. I know of no such school of health, now in existence, for teaching of this kind as would be started at Buckingham, if this project is carried out. And if carried out successfully, Buckingham may become a centre of supply of trained Health Missionaries – not only for its immediate neighbourhood only, but for many parts of England where such work is sorely needed.' Florence concluded by wishing North Bucks, 'distinguish itself by its wisdom and success in giving such an education to rural mothers, and in waging the war against national deterioration of health and vigour.'

Indeed, by May 1892, North Bucks in the capable hands of Dr De'Ath did distinguish itself by providing a quite remarkable training system of comprehensive lectures and an examination paper which he gave to sixteen ladies who wanted to be Rural Health Missioners but also around 70 other ladies attended out of personal interest to learn more about sanitation issues and Florence Nightingale's claim that 'Life or Death may lie in a grain of dust or a drop of water'. In a letter to Dr De'Ath dated 13th October 1892 written from Claydon House, she said, 'I give you joy with all my heart and soul at the success of your opening Lady Lectures – especially as it appears that at least Miss Bartlett had so many invitations to visit cottages. This is capital. Go on and prosper. God bless your work. I hope the Lady Missioners always report to you how many invitations they have had to Cottages'.

Then in a section she headed 'Private' and showing her faith in Dr De'Ath by seeking his advice, she added,

'Could you give us a simple wholesome way for Cottage Mothers to *stop up the gaping chinks* between boards of floor? Tow and red lead is recommended – but babies might find red lead dangerous. Tow and tar is messy. What is the best thing? May all your measure prove successful. But we must not expect too much *practical* progress at first.

Yours ever sincerely,
F. Nightingale'

FLORENCE NIGHTINGALE & GEORGE H. DE'ATH

Dr De'Ath did expect a great deal and worked far too hard for his health to make these plans come true. Margaret Verney recorded, 'Death came to him at the age of thirty-nine, hastened by the over strain of continual work. But his example is one of those influences which raise and build up the whole community'. Dr De'Ath had built up the community desire for healthy and sanitary living, whilst Florence had been building up an international movement towards the same goals; two heroes in perfect accord.

Florence, who had become more and more bedridden, continued to stay for prolonged periods at Claydon House, throwing herself behind all manner of local schemes to improve rural education, health and happiness. She became involved in the idea to provide a Village Free Library in the Claydons and she personally donated £50 towards buying books for Steeple Claydon.

This extraordinary pioneer of so many beneficial developments for health and well-being did not confine her thoughts solely to assisting people. She delighted the children of Claydon House with the most entertaining and story-like notes sent from the confines of her bed. They would receive these pencil messages from Aunt Florence urging them to suspend mutton bones outside to help the birds get through the winter months. She would say, 'The Tom-tits have sent to me a Deputation headed by the little one who, if it were to take off its clothes, would find a roomy dwelling in a walnut. They state that two gigantic black parties, called, they believe, rooks, have feloniously carried off their two best bones – Haste for thy life, post, haste.' (M. Verney, *Bucks Biographies*, 1912)

Florence Nightingale, the perfect mixture of kindness, determination, and remarkable foresight, passed away in her ninetieth year, on 13th August 1910. She was mourned by so many across the world but also they rejoiced in her many

BUCKINGHAMSHIRE HEROES

achievements. One of the most fitting epitaphs for this heroic woman was contained in a letter written to her by her friend Benjamin Jowett in 1879, at a time when she was having to take more and more to her bed through sickness. He wrote: 'There was a great deal of romantic feeling about you 23 years ago when you returned home from the Crimea . . . and now you work on in silence, and nobody knows how many lives are saved by your nurses in hospitals; how many thousand soldiers . . . are now alive owing to your forethought and diligence; how many natives of India in this generation and in generations to come have been preserved from famine and oppression and the load of debt by the energy of a sick lady who can scarcely rise from her bed. The world does not know all this or think about it. But I know it and often think about it.' *(Letter to Florence from Benjamin Jowett 31st December 1879.)*

In her Buckinghamshire days when she pioneered the Health Missioner scheme in Buckingham, she prepared a letter for the visiting ladies to show or read to her 'Bucks Cottage Mothers'. It began,

> 'Dear Hard-working friends,
> I am a hard-working woman too
> May I speak to you?
> And will you excuse me tho' not a mother?

Indeed she was a mother. A Buckinghamshire hero and 'Mother-Chief.'

———◆———

5

Ken 'Snakehips' Johnson (1914–1941)

'On the side of the street that's sunny'

The hero of this story is not Buckinghamshire born, nor was his short-lived fame lived out in this county, yet Kenrick Reginald Huymans Johnson from British Guiana left behind a Buckinghamshire legacy and a special status as an adopted county hero. Indeed, Wednesday 6th May 1998, saw the unveiling of a commemorative plaque on the West Street wall of Sir William Borlase's Grammar School in Marlow. It is dedicated to Ken 'Snakehips' Johnson.

To understand why a village grammar school in Buckinghamshire now pays tribute to a young man from British Guiana who passed so briefly through its studded oak doors is to discover a character that was destined to achieve so much, yet died in tragic circumstances before all could be realized.

It was 1929 and fresh from studying at Queen's College in British Guiana, Kenrick's parents decided that their 15-year-old son should finish his education at a private school in England. They chose Sir William Borlase's Grammar School and so it was that this 6 ft 4 ins tall, shy, boy with his dazzling smile turned up at school dressed in a memorable style. His father, a prominent doctor, had provided him with clothes more appropriate to his own university days in the early part of the 20th century than the fashionable 1920s. His green tweed knickerbockers and Norfolk jacket made quite an impression when contrasted with his peers wearing grey flannel trousers and school blazer. He was also the first and only black student in the school at that time, and for many, both in the school and village of Marlow, the very first Guianese person they had ever seen. For him to slip quietly into local school life was not a possibility.

Ken was certainly destined to create fashion statements later in life, but for now it was a trip down to Walter Davis, Marlow's school outfitters for the standard school uniform. Ken was a popular boy. In fact, his contemporaries felt he was rather special – he was someone to talk about not in a disparaging way but almost to show him off as belonging to Borlase rather than another school. They were proud of him.

His school friends, now used to this extraordinarily tall striking lad, loved to see the reaction of others when they played home or away at football. As goalkeeper for the first eleven football team, he could put on a very formidable appearance – framed at the far-end of the pitch he seemed a giant of a man daring the

Ken Johnson with the rest of the cricket team at Sir William Borlase's Grammar School in Marlow, 1930/31.

opposing team to even think of putting the ball past his athletic frame; although of course they did, as it was more bluff than anything else in his early days of football prowess. His good friend Wiggy, (George Wigmore) playing left half received the following report: 'Quickly settled down; his inclusion had no small share in the improvement on the left wing.'

By contrast, Ken was still learning his game and *The Borlasian* reported that he, 'Started the season very shakily, but has improved and is now much more reliable. Is inclined to hold the ball instead of punting it up the field.' (*The Borlasian* December 1929). By the following season both pals were 'much-improved' players and were to remain good friends after their school days. Ken went on to gain his 'first eleven colours' for cricket in his final school year of 1931.

However, his great passion was music and dancing. It was the era of exhibition dancing, with icons such as Fred Astaire, Bill 'Bojangles' Robinson and Earl 'Snakehips' Tucker who created the memorable 'shimmy', something Ken loved to imitate but adding and developing his own style.

Edna Foreman whose ex-army father, known as 'Sergeant' to the boys, and who taught physical education, lived at the school house with her mother who was Matron and her elder sister Gwen. Edna recalled, 'At the end of each term, the boarders would be given the choice of a visit to the local cinema . . . or a party (*which*) . . . was the usual preference and we all had to do a party piece. This is when Ken came into his own, entertaining us with his agile dancing, hips rotating in an amazing fashion, singing while standing at the piano strumming the odd notes.' (*The Borlasian*, 1991, p18)

It wasn't the piano he is remembered for during his school days but the violin. Ken was persuaded to play the hymns in the School Chapel at morning assembly, accompanying the organist, Billy Birkett. Former school chum, Ron Compton, recalls seeing him dash past, violin case in his hand, on his way to the Chapel. He also recalls he was not the best of players.

Ken was a charismatic character, a person with genuine charm and concern for others which made him liked by all. Again, Edna recalled, 'My mother was in charge at one particular supper time and sat at the head of the dining table. The boys, for a lark, no doubt, started to converse in French which my mother didn't understand. She left the room. There was a general hush, followed by great whisperings. Apart from being very fond of my mother, and regretting their behaviour, I suspect they were more than a little worried about the Sergeant getting to hear of it. Ken took the matter into his own hands, sought out my mother, no doubt apologizing and brought her back into the dining hall. Not another word was mentioned of this incident.' (*The Borlasian*, p18)

The Sergeant was not someone to cross, yet Ken had a cheeky trick that charmed all who knew about it, which must have included the Sergeant who chose to ignore it. Ron recalls that when the boys set off walking the mile or so to Quarry Woods pool for swimming lessons, they would pass a butcher's shop. Ken had already made the butcher's acquaintance so when he saw the butcher's delivery bike left outside the shop, he'd ask to borrow it. Given the okay, off he'd pedal to the delight of his peers, sometimes with Wiggy or another friend perched in the basket on the front. They would be down at Quarry Woods way before the others. The illicit bike-ride was the best bit for Ken as he was neither a great swimmer nor lover of cold water but he did persevere and obtain his school swimming certificate.

Whilst boarding school life in this small Buckinghamshire village continued for Ken, two sets of plans were formulating for his future, plus a third that took even Ken by surprise. Firstly, Ken's parents had clearly decided that when he left his English schooling, he should return to British Guiana to study medicine.

His father was, after all, a doctor and Minister of Health and this was a fitting career for his son. Ken, however, harboured the second set of plans which he knew would not make his parents happy. He wanted to be a dancer, a tap dancer, an exhibition dancer; whatever was possible but a first-class dancer, come what may.

He was seventeen when he left Borlase in 1931, supposedly to go back and study in Giuana, although Edinburgh University was discussed, but he had an overwhelming passion to go on tour as a dancer in a revue of some kind. He was tall, handsome, very supple and self-taught, but determined to seek lessons. Ken also knew he would not pass his exams to get into university, whereas his chum Wiggy was on his way to a very creditable performance in his School Certificate and Ron had already left with excellent results in his. Because Ken was engaged in his own very secretive plans to enter show business during this time, the only clues to his movements, and, it seems, early successes, are contained in a recently discovered letter to George Wigmore in which Ken speaks of already working in a touring revue, throwing parties and living at a W.1. London address:

> 43 Bernard Street
> Russell Square
> London W.C.1
> 10/4/31

Dear Wiggy,

This address will probably surprise you very much. I awfully sorry I could not answer your letter but not being in Dutch Guiana, I did not receive it until about a month ago. You see I was touring Manchester, Liverpool etc. in a review. So I only got all my letters when I returned back to London. What happened was that I spent two weeks at home & then my mother said that I should come back to go to school in case I failed.

Of course I knew I was bound to fail. So I persuaded her to let me leave home before the results arrived. So I was back in England in October. I then went to a School of Tap and Stage dancing & singing & now lo and behold according to Gravy* I am on the stage. By the way I have got a free week this week. Some of my friends and I are throwing a dance on Saturday night it starts at 11.30pm and finishing at 8am or thereabouts.

Would you like to come. I'll put you up. Try and come in the morning & we go & see some shows. Tell me what train you are coming down on & I'll be there to meet you or if you like why not come down by Skylark.

I'll have lots to tell you when you come down. Now try your very best to come down on next Saturday. Write & let me know immediately if you can come then & I can make arrangements for putting . . .

By the way don't mention to anyone that I wrote as I haven't written to Sgt and he doesn't known that I am in England. Remember me to Betty and your people. Cheerio,

All the best

Johnnie

(Ken Johnson)

Don't forget to write pronto.'

This letter, (reproduced just as it was written) so clearly shows Ken's plan to stave off the family pressure to achieve qualifications whilst at the same time and as fast as he possibly could, take up dancing and star in revues. The reference to *Gravy is to Canon Graves who taught religious knowledge and who predicted, quite accurately as it turned out, that Ken was destined for the stage one day. Although he'd now left school, he was concerned that Sgt (Sergeant) shouldn't be offended that he was in England but not in touch with his old mentor. Betty was George's sister. Ken was truly on his way to a remarkable period of stardom yet his association with Borlase was to remain strong and he was destined to return there but, unfortunately, in tragic circumstances.

Swing was the music he loved and musical stage shows of all shades. Ken's invitation to Wiggy to see some London shows would have no doubt taken in those currently storming the West End under the brilliant partnership of legendary impresario C.B.Cochran working with Noel Coward's genius, such as the 1931 *Revue* and *Cavalcade*. Also, multi-instrumentalist Leslie Thompson was at his most prominent at this time, particularly revered as a swing and stage musical trumpeter and he had passionate plans to form an all black dance band. It was Thompson's plans that would soon catch up with an enthusiastic Ken Johnson presenting him with the surprise career move that made him famous.

Andy Simons, formerly Jazz Curator at the British Library Sound Archive and now Social History Curator in the Modern British Collections, refers to Thompson's 'hot jazz experience' and reminds us not only of his undoubted influence on the young Ken Johnson but also the other possibilities now close by in the London of the 1930s. He adds in a key piece of the Ken 'Snakehips' jigsaw by noting that African American choreographer Clarence 'Buddy' Bradley, who had already taught Fred Astaire and other Hollywood screen dancers, was in London at that time: 'C.B. Cochran lured Bradley and his partner Billy Pearce from the States to set up a studio in Compton Street, Clerkenwell, and they transformed London's stage and screen dance by giving it a fluid, less tethered-to-one-spot quality.'

Ken was excited about his show-business future and his reference to Wiggy about attending a School of Tap and Stage

BUCKINGHAMSHIRE HEROES

Dancing and Singing was, no doubt, that very same Compton Street studio run by Buddy Bradley. His fast track journey to cabaret and revue had begun but there was much more in store for Ken than even he could realize. He made enough money in revue work to travel to the States to look up contacts he had been given whilst in the UK.

By 1934/5, only a few years after leaving Borlase, he made some short dancing films for Warner Brothers. He had perfected his hip-swivelling movements from a party piece at Borlase School to quite a spectacular and mesmerising degree that made him stand out amongst his dancing peers. Back in England at Michael Balcon's famous Gainsborough Pictures, he was snapped up for a dancing role in a 1935 film called *Oh Daddy*. Not bad for a young man, now only four years out of Borlase, and determined to entertain. His dream was more than coming true and there were even better days and more surprises to come.

It was through Leslie Thompson's gargantuan efforts and Ken Johnson's sheer dancing charisma, that by 1936, they had created the Johnson Orchestra. There were many musicians eager for work and Thompson had soon realized the draw of such an attractive and versatile front man as Ken Johnson. Indeed, the name and composition of 'Snakehips' Orchestra would alternate on the billing, The Aristocrats of Jazz, or The Emperors of Swing or even The (Jamaican) Emperors of Jazz. What would not alternate was the prominent position of one Ken 'Snakehips' Johnson.

Ken also remembered his school and with his new status as dance band leader would make the occasional visit to what he saw as his first English home.

Ken Johnson was not a musician as such, but he was an entertainer and a guarantee for a good night out, what was then called 'a hot night out'. The sheer spectacle of the band in full swing and Ken in even more swinging mood would draw the crowds, particularly the ladies who loved his elegant evening

KEN 'SNAKEHIPS' JOHNSON

Ken 'Snakehips' Johnson.

dress style and smooth dance moves. A lot of the early work, however, was not in clubs but music halls, cinemas and occasional radio broadcasts. The best was yet to come.

By 1937, Ken formed a partnership with his manager Ralph Deene for joint ownership of the Orchestra – they were poised on a breakthrough residency which they won at The Old Florida Club, Bruton Mews in London's West End. This brought them to the attention of a BBC producer Leslie Perowne who used them at the famous Shepherd's Bush Empire from where the BBC broadcast live shows. Johnson set about hiring the best of the black musicians around, and they were just as keen to join 'Snakehips'. Andy Simons concludes,'The quality of newcomers helped maintain the Johnson band's reputation as superlative swingers.'

Their residency at The Old Florida Club was a major London attraction for the late crowd who loved the revolving dance floor but the 'revolving' Ken 'Snakehips' Johnson even more as the band took the stage around 2 am. Other residences followed but it was the 1939 one that was the icing on the cake – the Cafe de Paris, just off Leicester Square.

By this time, Ken was also quite a proficient conductor and this added even more flair to his performance and status as band leader. Ken's aspirations could now legitimately soar to thoughts of international fame, perhaps even performing at the New York World Fair. What he did do, however, was take his band down to the Crown Hotel at Marlow to play for his old school chums – The Borlasians. Ron Compton, who had been in Ken's form at school, was there, and it was just a magnificent evening. 'Ken never forgot his school', he told me.

What Ken had now achieved through his key selection of top musicians were two British firsts. Not only was he the first British black dance band leader, but now he was fronting the very first West Indian Dance Orchestra.The billing that was to finally cement his fame and his remarkable achievements was,

Ken 'Snakehips' Johnson
& His West Indian Dance Orchestra

Already Decca records had put out his very own, *Snakehips Swing*, whilst his signature tune became a re-working of *On the Sunny Side of the Street'*, his own swing version entitled *On the Side of the Street That's Sunny*.

It was Saturday 8th March 1941, in wartime London. Despite this, there was plenty of night life, albeit without the beckoning neon lights. Tucked down into the basement of the Cafe de Paris which proclaimed itself, 'the safest restaurant in London', was the restaurant and dance floor where people flocked to see 'Snakehips'.

Indeed, one of our other Buckinghamshire heroes, Sir John Mills, who had been struggling with a distinctly 'out-of-character' part as a German spy in *Cottage to Let*, recalled that very Saturday in March: 'After the last day's shooting, Mary and I decided to celebrate the fact that I had managed to finish the epic. I booked a table at the Cafe de Paris, where there was always a good cabaret and Snakehips Johnson was in permanent residence.'

In the event, he couldn't say why, but something made him change his mind and they went for a walk instead, getting caught in an air-raid which saw them sheltering (probably unwisely) under a tree by the Serpentine helplessly watching London's West End being bombed. Above the Cafe de Paris was the empty Rialto Cinema and this took a direct hit from two bombs which tore into the building, smashing down through the floor into the basement.

Wartime reporting restrictions meant that details of where London had taken a hit and the casualties and any other details were very sparse and would not necessarily be reported immediately. However, anyone, particularly John and Mary Mills reading *The Times* of Monday, 10th March 1941, were given all the clues they needed to know about the horror of what had occurred.

The cautious *Times* of Monday 10th March 1941 reported: 'In the bright moonlight of Saturday night, London had its heaviest air attack for some weeks. It was a noisy night. For some time the throbbing of aircraft never ceased. Nor did the guns; the biggest barrage for some time was put up . . . Outstanding gallantry was shown by the diners and dancers in a restaurant which was wrecked by a high-explosive bomb. It was filled with a gay crowd on Saturday evening, many in uniform. The lively band had opened its programme and the floor was crowded with dancers, "Oh Johnny," the band was playing, while outside the guns crashed, but here unheard against the accompaniment of cheerful music and chatter. Then suddenly there was an explosion somewhere above, the ceiling fell in and all but one of the lights went out. The restaurant was filled with dust and fumes, which blackened faces and frocks. Couples dancing had been flung apart; those able to do so struggled to their feet and many searched amid the confusion with torches and lighted matches for their partner of a second before. Many had been killed; others were seriously hurt.'

The article goes on in almost light-hearted vein to speak of 'wonderful escapes' and many with a few cuts or bruises. 'Oh Johnny,' was the clue that told everyone Ken Johnson was on stage at the time which also meant it must be the Cafe de Paris. What the reports could not say was that 30 people lay dead, amongst them Ken 'Snakehips' Johnson who was fatally wounded, dying in the ambulance on the way to hospital. Reports claim he lay unmarked, immaculately dressed as usual, with a perfect red carnation in his button-hole.

Aged 26 and poised to reach so many other musical peaks, all was shattered amongst the debris and death of that fateful night. It was the reporting of the incident by the *Bucks Free Press* that Friday that brought home the tragedy of what had occurred. Under the banner, 'Old Borlasian Killed by Bomb' it also reminded us of the Buckinghamshire legacy of another swing band playing with Ken that night, Nat Allen from High Wycombe who fortunately escaped serious injury. The report reminds us of the quite remarkable achievement of Ken in that all of the West Indies were represented in his orchestra and it goes on to say: 'He always retained a high regard for Borlase and regularly attended their annual dinners.' Borlase, in return, had a high regard for Ken and sadly Ken's last visit to the school was for a memorial service in his honour exactly one year from his death. On 8th March 1942, his ashes were transferred from Golders Green

KEN 'SNAKEHIPS' JOHNSON

cemetery and laid to rest in the School Chapel behind a decorative panel.

On 8th March 1991 to celebrate the 50th anniversary of Ken's substantial legacy to the world of Black British Swing and his affection for his adopted county, Sir William Borlase's Grammar School held a magnificent jazz night in his memory and featured Will Gaines tap dancing in Ken's honour. Ken would be absolutely over the moon to know that the celebration of his life and his legacy is still remembered at School Prize-giving Day. The Ken 'Snakehips' Johnson prize for jazz improvisation is awarded to a pupil involved with the thriving jazz band tradition that has now evolved at his old school and who is seen as deserving of recognition for that year's work.

Finally, Ken's commemorative plaque (shown above) on the West Street wall of Sir William Borlase's Grammar School in Marlow is, as I noted on a recent summer visit to photograph it, definitely

'On the side of the street that's sunny.'

6

Thomas Ball (1989–2003)

'I've not done anything, only been ill.'

'Tom had an incredible sense of humour. He always saw the
funny side of everything. I don't know how he did.'
(Elaine Ball)

Some heroes tug at your heart strings and young
Buckinghamshire hero, Thomas Ball, does just that.
Prestwood lad, Thomas lost his life, at age fourteen on
Monday 30th June 2003 at 12.25 am. At home on his favourite
settee, with his beloved dog Pip and with his family beside him,
his long, courageous and memorable fight against neuroblastoma ended.

But, this rare childhood cancer, which so tragically took
Thomas, and affects around 80 to 90 children a year in the UK,
is still being fought thanks to Tom's legacy – the Thomas Ball
Children's Cancer Fund. His remarkable story is inspirational in
its contribution, not only to fighting a serious childhood illness,
but to absolute selflessness and a dedicated concern for others.

It was January 1997. Seven-year-old Tom had been
uncharacteristically quiet over the Christmas period. A lively,
even hyper-active boy, the contrast was marked. He complained
of backache, not feeling right. Local doctor's visits followed, but
no satisfactory answer was found to Tom's condition. At school,
they too noticed a difference, particularly in the PE lessons. Tom
wasn't moving with the usual ease of one who was now an
eight-year-old, happy-go-lucky lad; Tom's usual demeanour. His

THOMAS BALL (1989–2003)

three sisters, Cathy, Ceri and Clare certainly saw a change when the normal brother-sister feuds diminished significantly.

This led to Tom being referred to a Co-ordination Clinic in Amersham. They assessed him eating, they assessed him socialising, they assessed him playing, drawing, all kinds of situations were evaluated, and Tom turned out about what would be expected for a child of his age. Perhaps a few tweaks here and there such as some speech therapy or occupational therapy would be beneficial, but nothing out of the ordinary. His gait needed some attention and so it was that Tom and his mother ended up seeing an orthopaedic surgeon. Here, many weeks down the line, some progress seemed possible – his hips, declared the consultant, were like a baby's – they had not developed to those expected in an eight-year-old lad.

Tom, however, had been experiencing terribly high temperatures and, in his fever, he would be in great pain. This was more than malformed hip bones, but still there had been no x-rays, no blood tests, so whatever was going on inside young Tom was not visible to even the expert's eye. Also, his naturally lively and mischievous side would re-emerge as soon as the fever left him, so it was tricky for the medics to catch him at the critical moment to pass their opinion.

It was a paediatrician who asked Tom's mum to bring him in, by-passing the GP, as soon as Tom had a feverish episode. A blood test showed he was anaemic but it was only after the CT scan that the serious nature of Tom's condition was revealed. Elaine Ball, Tom's mum recalls, 'So we were rushed into Wycombe Hospital for tests. By the time we got into the hospital, he'd got over the episode and he was bouncing around on the window sill, jumping on the bed and making me feel embarrassed that we were there at all because there were all these sick children and I'm saying "Be quiet there's all these sick children around," you know, and, "You've got to behave yourself," and he's jumping around all over the place. That's the trouble with neuroblastoma, it comes and goes you see, that's the thing, that's why it's so hard for doctors to diagnose it.

They whipped him through the CT scanner and then they told us we had to go into a private room. And I'm saying. "Oh that's alright there's people over there that are a lot worse off than us – put them in the private room". I didn't realise they were trying to get us to one side to break the news to us that he had got cancer. So, anyway we got into this room and then we got called into the office and he's still bouncing around on the bed, on the window sill and everything, playing with surgical gloves, syringes and stuff, and they just dropped the bombshell – my wedding anniversary as well in 1997 – just dropped the bombshell that he had got cancer and they said it was neuroblastoma. They knew he had got it on his adrenal gland – it was the type of cancer that was very aggressive and would probably have spread but until we were sent over to Oxford for further tests they didn't know the extent of the spread. So, we get him home, for about two days, gathered stuff together and everything, then we went over to Oxford and then our feet never touched the ground. But when we got home, he went out and mowed the lawn and we're thinking when we go back to Oxford we are bound to get good news, it can't possibly have spread because he's mowing the lawn. But when we got over there for the results, they said it was all in his bones, it was in his ribs, in his knees, in his pelvis, it was right through to the core of his bone marrow.'

Two important features emerge from Elaine's account of this terrible time. Firstly, the concern for other people who were 'worse off' which was to become Tom's focus for the rest of his short but busy life that turned a sick child, often in severe pain, into a pioneer hero for others whom he always put before himself; secondly, the sheer horror of the destructive speed of this disease which has such poor prognosis. Although the survival rate

THOMAS BALL (1989–2003)

is about 25%, Tom was already at stage 4 which indicated a much reduced chance of survival. Whilst chemotherapy and surgery can be successful, it often re-occurs and the prognosis when that happens is terminal.

Tom knew his condition, and would comfort his mum by saying,

'Well, mum, people die of the flu, you know.'

This terrible news for Tom's family had quite a remarkable effect on Tom himself. His concern for others, which had always been a feature of his character, took on a new impetus. He would now see other sick children on the ward where he was being treated and discover they were in danger of dying and this would worry him and he wanted to help. It didn't have to be a child or a terminal illness that concerned him. People coping with the pain from arthritic conditions upset him, young people with cystic fibrosis. His focus became one of asking how he could help them despite his own very serious and painful condition.

Tom's condition was such that it saw him undergoing eleven courses of chemotherapy, enduring over 100 blood and platelet transfusions, as well as major surgery, in an attempt to remove the primary tumor, including undergoing a stem cell transplant which meant almost three months in an isolation cubicle.

As his treatment continued over a 21-month period, Tom made every effort to attend school as regularly as possible and be his own lively self when the neuroblastoma and his debilitating treatment allowed. However, it was difficult for Tom to keep a regular school and social life, whilst suffering so many sessions of chemotherapy.

His ideas to help others came from his own family's experience when considering a family holiday. Tom's condition meant that he couldn't travel abroad, nor plan a simple week's break in the UK. His illness had such an unpredictable character that he had to be close to specialist help and so any proposed holiday might

BUCKINGHAMSHIRE HEROES

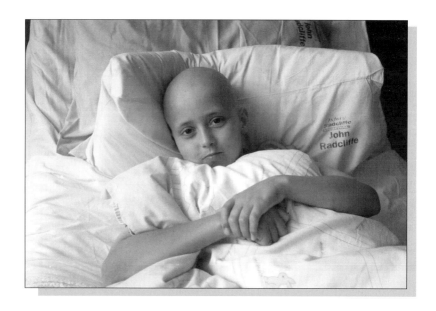

*Being treated in isolation at the John Radcliffe Hospital
in Oxford in August 1998.*

have to be cancelled at the last minute. Charitable assistance was possible to cater for such family breaks with a seriously ill young person, but the waiting list was long. All through his illness he thought long and hard about his first venture into helping others who were ill. 'Wouldn't it be a good thing', reported Tom, to dad Trevor and mum Elaine, 'if we got somewhere where children who were ill could go and have a holiday?' With that decided, he announced he was holding a fete in the back garden of his Prestwood home to raise money for that very purpose. His mum recalls, 'I said, "Don't be so silly", and he kept on and on about it, so I said, "Oh let's just put a few stalls up because he's so ill and it will amuse him and it might shut him up."' She laughs at the memory. 'Well it didn't shut him up because he made about £500 and then he said "Oh, why don't we do a bike ride?" And

THOMAS BALL (1989-2003)

Thomas, with one of his heroes, Gianfranco Zola, during his treatment in 1998.

it was just one thing after another.'

During the first few months of 1999, Tom was improving and it seemed possible that the severe treatment regime had worked. Tom appeared to be getting fitter and so the sponsored bike ride went ahead from Holmer Green to Prestwood in April 1999.

Together with his friends, he raised £1,700 for research into neuroblastoma. Tom was now hooked on helping others and went on raising money. A sponsored swim put another £2,700 into the kitty to purchase play and medical equipment for Wycombe General Hospital. Lots of fund-raising initiatives continued and by November 1999, the 'Thomas Ball Children's Cancer Fund' was officially set up to make the most of willing local support towards such a good cause and a great ambassador, Tom Ball aged ten. Lots of fund-raising work continued, with Tom spearheading the initiatives, be they disco dances, barbecues, fetes or fun sponsorship ideas.

All the while, Tom continued nursing his very special dream. He wanted money to buy a seaside caravan where sick children could have a holiday. Tom and his family toured around different seaside locations looking at battered old caravans, which were quite unsuitable, but the money raised for this project was limited and Tom was not going to give up. More money had to be found.

*Tom doing a sponsored swim in January 2000 to raise money
for other children with cancer.*

Also Tom had now set his sights on a seaside chalet rather than a
caravan. An appeal to John Lewis's High Wycombe Charities
Committee for funds for £3,000 clinched it and Tom's dream was
fast becoming a reality.

Autumn 2001 was so special for Tom. He was still in remission,
he was catching up with his school work, and everyone was
hoping his intensive and painful treatment over the past years
had yielded the much hoped for result. Now here he was
standing outside a two bedroomed holiday chalet at Naish, near
New Milton in Hampshire, on a lovely sunny Saturday. Close to
the seaside at Bournemouth and the exciting New Forest ponies,
this was not any old chalet. As he cut the ribbon and the corks
popped, this was named officially, 'Tom's Retreat'.

THOMAS BALL (1989–2003)

Here it was for real – a holiday home chosen by Tom that would be made available, free of charge, to families where a child in that family had been diagnosed with cancer or leukaemia. During its first season over 20 families enjoyed using it for a much-needed break. Tom had really made quite an amazing positive difference to so many lives where serious illness had taken so much away. Tom, through the charity that bears his name, would do all he could to lift the spirits of other sick children. A young boy dying from leukaemia had always wanted a motorbike. Much to the horror of the Great Ormond Hospital consultant, Tom arranged for this boy's dream to come true. He bought him a motorbike, something he had always secretly wanted for himself, and he eventually saved up his own money to do just that.

The year 2002 began with Tom relishing his new life away from the debilitating treatment regimes. He was in good spirits and looking forward to more local fund-raising schemes for the charity. He was a very proficient disc jockey and would regularly DJ at local fund-raising fun evenings. School work was good and he had been commended on his progress. Trevor and Elaine were so hopeful for their son's future. Elaine wrote of that time, 'Could the nightmare finally be over?' After all, everything appeared normal.

It was now five years on since the January aches and pains of 1997 that brought Tom and his family that terrible news of his advanced condition of neuroblastoma. It was January once more and Tom was busy with his homework.

Tom called out, 'Mum, what's this lump in my neck?' Elaine recalls, 'I froze on the spot when he showed me the swelling. A visit to the GP the next day put us at ease. "It's only a gland from a sore throat," we were informed.'

The hospital consultant knew otherwise, the bombshell they all prayed had moved on, was dropped again as the cancer was located in Tom's lymph nodes. Tom's damaged bone marrow from previous treatments meant the chemotherapy treatment had to be scaled down, but by September 2002 he had to endure the alternative MIBG, a radioactive-based treatment that kept him in isolation. His sense of humour, however, was never in isolation throughout this ordeal. It was Tom who kept the family positive.

His remarkable achievements were officially commended in October 2002 when the Lord Lieutenant of Buckinghamshire, Sir Nigel Mobbs, presented Tom with a Queen's Golden Jubilee Award: Young Achiever Award 2002. Tom, in great pain, smiled and graciously accepted this reward given to symbolise his outstanding courage and determination to help others, despite his own personal struggle.

For Tom, being ill should have been a thing of the past after all the treatments he had endured. He wanted more time and strength to continue his fund-raising for others and he had every right to be angry at the turn of events that was now weakening him once more. But he wasn't, he was just determined to get better.

Spring 2003 saw Tom in a much weakened state – there is no protocol for dealing with neuroblastoma once a child relapses. His youngest sister Clare, now 20, could not face what all the family now knew – Tom was dying – and the doctors had no treatment regime left for him. She set about planning to raise money from a sponsored parachute jump to try and raise funds for a specialist consultation in America where new treatments might be possible. Tom, of course, could not receive financial support from the charity in his own name – new monies were needed.

Whilst Clare drummed up support for her June jump, Tom's school had nominated him for a Diana Princess of Wales Memorial Award for Young People. It was a total surprise and scheduled for a presentation at the school on 20th March 2003, just after Tom's 14th birthday. Elaine recalls, 'He was so ill that day. It was when we knew there was no hope, he was definitely dying. He's doped up on morphine and we have got to get him

THOMAS BALL (1989–2003)

out of his bed and down to the Misbourne and he's posing for all those photographs. As soon as we got home he went straight back to bed. He was so ill that day but he just had to go and get it.' Tom's strength of character would not allow him other than to be there. The award was for his courage and being an outstanding role model to his peers – he showed it again that day. He said to the assembled crowd, 'I liked Princess Diana, she was nice but I've not done anything, only been ill.' Very few people, other than his family, would have realized how painful that journey had been for Tom.

By April, Tom was having more radioactive therapy just in case it could halt the progression of the disease. It seemed impossible. It was 1st June 2003 and the whole family went to Oxford to watch Clare undertake her sponsored parachute jump. Tom did not know this was just for him rather than for the charity. He loved it and Clare was spectacular. She raised almost £1,000 towards Tom's trip to America. Perhaps there was a way forward, now Clare had begun this new possibility on the first day of a new month for Tom.

It was not to be. Tom died on the very last day of that same month, 30th June 2003. He would have approved, though of the money Clare raised going to the Thomas Ball Children's Charity so that it could help others. After all, other people always needed help far more than Tom, a real Buckinghamshire hero.

****

Once when he was about six years old, his bicycle was flattened by an ice-cream van but Tom escaped unscathed and came home with the damaged bike announcing, 'Its alright, Mum, he gave me a ninety nine.'

7

John Hampden (1594–1643)

'. . . a gallant man, a kind man and an able man and for all I know, second to none to any living man.'
(Arthur Goodwin – Aylesbury constituency, 1643)

Why would 6,000 Buckinghamshire men endure a long and difficult journey to London to protest and petition their support of another Buckinghamshire man? In a complex and compelling tale of an unscrupulous king of England and a Parliament too weak to curb the king's financial excesses, his plotting, orders of assassination and imprisonment – one man stands out as championing the cause of his local people. He was John Hampden, an elected Member of Parliament for Wendover, as well as for Buckinghamshire, in the first half of the 17th century. With Charles I doing all he could to dispense with any form of Parliamentary scrutiny over his subversive, undemocratic and dictatorial activities, the people of the county as well as many across the country, fell in behind John Hampden's selfless fight to end the king's tyrannical behaviour and bring justice to the land.

You have possibly seen Henry C. Fehr's bronze statue to John Hampden in Aylesbury's Market Square, or the unusual stone cross dedicated to him standing by Prestwood's village boundary. You may even have supped a pint of John Hampden's ale brewed by the local Chiltern Brewery and wondered why this man's name is so prominent well over three and half centuries since his death. Aficionados of British horror movies of the late 1970s and early 1980s, made by Hammer Films will also have seen glimpses of John Hampden's Buckinghamshire family home and extensive

JOHN HAMPDEN (1594–1643)

John Hampden.
(R. Chamber, Book of Days)

grounds. The striking Gothic features of Hampden House were transformed into the *Hammer House of Horror* for both television and cinema entertainment.

John Hampden was born in 1594* and the legacy of this man's life is to be found in many locations other than Buckinghamshire. He attended Lord Williams's Grammar School, Thame, in the early 1600s. He went on to Magdalen College, Oxford, in 1609 and then, in 1613, to London, where he qualified as a lawyer at the Inner Temple. In quite an amazing coincidence for a man who was to become a political hero, when his mother moved to London, the 'new' Hampden House was on the site of what is now Downing Street. A fine statue of Hampden can also be found at the entrance to the Central Lobby of the House of Commons.

So, here we have a man, an older cousin of Oliver Cromwell no less, descended from a wealthy and ancient Buckinghamshire family and making his way in life with all the class and financial privileges at his fingertips that would be part and parcel of being born into the aristocracy of 17th-century England. So how did he end his days as a Buckinghamshire hero and earn the title 'Patriae Pater', the Father of the People?

---

*Following new research by the eminent English Civil War historian, Earl Russell, the *Dictionary of National Biography*, published by the OUP in 2004, puts his birth as about June 1595 but other authorities, including the John Hampden Society, have yet to debate this revised date.

BUCKINGHAMSHIRE HEROES

At least three landmark occasions for Hampden were to lead him down this path. Firstly, his marriage on 24th June 1619 to Elizabeth Simeon, daughter of Edmund Simeon of Pyrton Manor, Oxfordshire. It was a marriage that bore them nine children and he had a deep loving relationship with his family and fatherly concerns for their future happiness.

Secondly, following in the family tradition, he took a seat in Parliament in 1621. This was in James I's Parliament and it was not for Buckinghamshire but as a member for Grampound in Cornwall. It was here he learnt about the very deep clashes that existed between the whims and wishes of the monarchy and the powerful patronage and scheming of the landed gentry who dominated a Parliament reflecting their own values rather than that of the people. It was here he differed from other men of his class. They saw being a lawyer and Parliamentarian as advancing their own personal careers whereas Hampden saw the challenge of using wise counsel and oratory as a way of obtaining natural justice and balance. When James was forced to dissolve a Parliament that thwarted his wishes, John Hampden thought long and hard about the role of the sovereign and the rule of law. They were not balanced – the crown outweighed natural justice in a selfish and unscrupulous manner.

Hampden had his first clash with Royal anger when King James learnt that Hampden had uncovered a lapsed right for three Buckinghamshire boroughs to have Parliamentary representation. These were Amersham, Marlow and Wendover. James tried to stop it but Hampden secured House of Commons approval for the three boroughs and he himself became the member for Wendover. So began John Hampden's career as someone prepared to challenge the status quo in the name of rights and duties rather than self-interest. It was, however, under the Parliament of King Charles I that his fighting spirit and eventual heroic status was confirmed to this day.

JOHN HAMPDEN (1594–1643)

The third event was the death of his close friend Sir John Eliot some time later in 1632 under Charles's reign. Eliot had been imprisoned in the Tower in 1629 for putting a successful motion to the House that anyone paying forced loans demanded by the king was betraying the liberty of England. The king's revenge on Eliot for putting forward this motion and denying him the monies he had demanded was imprisonment in conditions that led to the onset of tuberculosis. The king's further refusal of medical treatment and access to fresh air lead to Eliot's certain death and John Hampden would not forgive the king for the murder of his friend.

Prior to this terrible event for Hampden, he had been no stranger to imprisonment himself. It was during the Parliament of 1625 that established how unscrupulous Charles was going to be against a House of Commons that was digging its heels in against his unreasonable, personal financial demands. It was a Parliament justly trying to bring to task certain individuals such as the Lord High Admiral George Villiers, First Duke of Buckingham, who was also raising taxes and appropriating funds for abortive and ill-advised naval engagements and generally undermining the whole administrative structure of the British navy.

In the second Parliament of 1626, the House of Commons was determined to stop the monarchy dissolving Parliament every time it tried to control the king's actions and unlawful ambitions by passing what was called a Remonstrance. This was a list of complaints and objections about the king's undemocratic behaviour.

Charles, true to form, promptly dissolved Parliament and ordered the Remonstrance burnt. He then went on to demand money by imposing a forced loan on the country. Charles required money and it was to be raised from key Parliamentarians and others he pointed the finger at across the kingdom. This was ruled illegal by the Chief Justice, who immediately lost his job as a consequence. John Hampden refused to pay this unlawful demand and had to repeat his refusal before the Privy Council. Others, around 27, followed suit.

For his actions, Hampden initially was imprisoned in the Gatehouse Prison, Westminster, a dank, rat-infested place that caused his health to deteriorate. He was later kept under less stringent conditions in Hampshire. Although this was a harsh lesson in the power of the monarchy's ability to ride rough-shod over the democratic process, John Hampden was as determined as ever to bring justice and fair play to the political arena of the time. The test of his stoicism was to come in the momentous stand he took against what was termed Ship Money. However, the subsequent imprisonment of his good friend Eliot in 1629 and his tragic death in 1632 and the fact that Charles had dissolved Parliament for good as far as anyone could tell, seriously made John Hampden think about emigrating to America with his younger cousin Oliver Cromwell. How the course of history would have changed had they done so, can only be guessed at.

It was 1634 and Hampden had worked tirelessly to establish himself as a fair and honest Parliamentarian and Justice of the Peace. He was revered and trusted except by the enemies of fair play. Two disparate and serious events happened in that year. It was his fifteenth wedding anniversary on 24th June but no sooner had this happy occasion been celebrated by all, than his wife Elizabeth died. It is said she died in childbirth. John Hampden became mother and father to his nine children all under thirteen years of age. He grieved deeply over the loss of his beloved Elizabeth. The second event that was eventually to challenge him on the national political stage was the continuing unbounded extravagances of Charles I who was seeking more and more money to fund his royal life-style.

JOHN HAMPDEN (1594–1643)

In October of that same year, the king revived a redundant tax levy originally used for fighting the Spanish Armada in Elizabeth I's reign, the so-called Ship Tax. The country was being governed solely by the king; there was no Parliamentary authority, no checks or balances. The Ship Tax was levied on maritime counties so it did not affect Buckinghamshire – yet!

It was unpopular and people who refused to pay suffered imprisonment, torture and even mutilation. Punishments meted out by the notorious Star Chamber of that time, in addition to whipping, pillorying and branding, were to order the offender's ears to be cut off and their noses slit. It was the autumn of the following year, 1635, that Charles extended the collection of this tax to inland counties on the basis that such money was needed for the defence of the realm.

Had the money been used for the country's benefit rather than for the king it may have made a difference but it was clearly money for his own coffers and John Hampden refused to pay the Buckinghamshire levy. The king had discovered a means of raising taxes without Parliamentary approval or discussion. To support such a means of funding the monarchy made him independent of Parliament and outside the democratic process. There was no future for Parliamentary democracy under this dictat and John Hampden chose to fight.

Great Kimble in Buckinghamshire listed 31 defaulters alongside John Hampden and he was also cited as defaulting on his Stoke Mandeville levy – the total sum demanded being around £20. It took until the new year for more writs to be issued against him for his refusal to pay and by October 1636, what may be termed in modern parlance, the 'final demand' was issued from the king for his money. The test case was to be his refusal to pay 20 shillings for his Stoke Mandeville estates. The law trundled on and it wasn't until November 1637 that it came to court. Could the king prove, as stated in the writs, that he needed to protect the country against pirates – hence a need to build ships with these taxes? It was a ludicrous claim, but then he was the monarch of which the Crown reminded all, 'He is the centre of us all, wherein we all as in his loins, should meet; he is the soul of this body, whose proper act is to command.' There was no hasty judgment forthcoming from the twelve judges hearing this test case, but a protracted judicial process over many months that produced a verdict of seven votes to five in favour of the king. This was a stark message to the king in itself that five Chief Justices dissented from his view. The others, in effect, had left it open for the king to demand anything he chose from his subjects. They had handed the king an open cheque book for his extravagances and Hampden was not about to sign a blank cheque. However, as he had lost in a court of law, he abided by the judicial decision but was now more determined than ever to fight the king's tyranny.

His stand against the king's demand for Ship Money brought his name to the fore of debates and arguments across the whole country. Hampden was now famous and became known affectionately as 'The Patriot.' Charles found it difficult to collect this highly unpopular tax and, in effect, Hampden's action had forced the king to recall Parliament after a gap of eleven years. It was 1640 and the king needed additional funds to finance an expedition to end Scottish religious revolt.

England itself was close to civil war. Subsequent events in Parliament strengthened Hampden's patriotic reputation as he stood firm against further royal demands for money and was highly admired for his ability to quell tempers in dangerous and occasionally life-threatening situations. For example, in a veritable hothouse of emotions and anger of the Parliament of 1641, when rebellion had broken out in Ireland amongst the Catholics, it was necessary for the House to authorize the formation and deployment of armed forces. However, they could

JOHN HAMPDEN (1594–1643)

not trust the king to have control of this army without severe conditions being laid down. In the dynamic and inflammatory atmosphere of a long night-time debate, Parliament managed to draw up what became known as the Grand Remonstrance.

Written in the same spirit as Magna Carta, but with considerably more haste, it clearly outlined all of their complaints against the king – including the death of Hampden's friend John Eliot, 'Whose blood still cries for revenge'. This was to put the king in his place with clear accounts of his misdeeds and warnings for the future that he would be required to heed. The electric atmosphere that night had both sides with hands poised on the pommels of their swords. A clash of blades was a mere cat's whisker away but for the guidance of John Hampden. It was said of that night by one member, 'I thought we had all sat in the valley of the shadow of death; for we, like Joab's and Abner's young men, had caught at each other's locks and sheathed our swords in each other's bowels had not the sagacity and great calmness of Mr Hampden, by a short speech, prevented it.'

Charles certainly wanted to sheath his sword in John Hampden's bowels and early the following year, 4th January 1642, broke every convention of the democratic process by heading up several hundred armed soldiers and marching from the Palace of Westminster into the House of Commons to personally arrest Hampden and other key figures in the House on charges of high treason. No monarch may enter the House but this king had no respect for ancient rights and privileges. Hampden and his colleagues had been warned and reluctantly left by a back exit onto the Thames. The king is recorded as saying, 'The birds have flown'.

Buckinghamshire pride ran high for John Hampden. During the eleven years when Parliament was dissolved, he had won much local admiration for his tireless local work as a Justice of the Peace and now his fight against the excesses of the monarchy on behalf of the people had touched many hearts and minds, locally and nationally.

John Hampden was a hero and, more than that, he was a Buckinghamshire hero; hence the sight of 6,000 Buckinghamshire men riding to London to celebrate that fact. As they rode, three abreast down Cheapside, in each hat was wedged a copy of the Grand Remonstrance. They also brought petitions to Parliament and to the king, part of which proclaimed: 'John Hampden, knight of our Shire, in whose loyalty we, his countrymen and neighbours have ever had good cause to confide.' Now it was time to fight and Hampden intended to do just that.

He led the Commons' proposals that the Militia, the Tower and other principal forts be held not by Charles but by the people through the democratic institution of Parliament. Of course Charles refused, and civil war was now guaranteed. Hampden was appointed to the Committee of Safety, the 17th-century equivalent of a modern War Cabinet.

In his capacity as Deputy Lieutenant for Buckinghamshire, Hampden, together with his good friend Arthur Goodwin, who represented Aylesbury, created the legendary 'Greencoats' regiment from amongst their Buckinghamshire tenants. The war for the control of the militia had begun.

It was the summer of 1642 and Hampden's first skirmish was to see off the Earl of Berkshire who was trying to recruit Royalist troops for Charles. Hampden was then involved in more confrontations with the king's Greencoats in August of that year, as he travelled northwards to prevent the Royalists' march south from Nottingham. However, Prince Rupert, the king's 22-year-old nephew, continued his steady march south, taking Oxford and then attacking Brentford on his way to take control of the capital. The gun-fire could be heard in Parliament. Hampden arrived at Brentford just in time to take charge of the situation

JOHN HAMPDEN (1594–1643)

and thwart Prince Rupert's plans. A further skirmish at Turnham Green left the Royalists retreating to Oxford.

Buckinghamshire's Hampden House now formed the front-line between the Royalists at Oxford and the Parliamentarians in London. The complexities of the many civil war battles to follow are vast and by the summer of 1643, spread across the country. We cannot do justice to their detail here but in a memorable battle, of 15th April 1643, Parliamentary forces, lead by Hampden, captured Reading. The main hope now was for the Parliamentarians to pin the king down in Oxford.

Hampden worked tirelessly in collaboration with the Earl of Essex, who was headquartered in Thame, to raise more troops. Many soldiers, if not dead or wounded, were suffering terribly from disease and Prince Rupert was making effective sorties out of Oxford to attack the Parliamentarians. Hampden was determined to stop him.

It was in the early hours of 18th June 1643 and Thame HQ was alerted that Royalists had reached Postcombe, killed Parliamentarian troops there and were now heading for Chinnor where Parliamentary dragoons were quartered. They were attacked, and left afire as Rupert made his way back to Oxford. At Thame, Hampden took command of Captain James Cross's troop. He had asked Cross, 'Will you follow me?' The reply was 'Yes, lead us.' It was Hampden's countryside and he was a respected and trusted leader so there was no hesitation as they set off in pursuit of the Royalists.

It was early that same morning at Chalgrove Field in Buckinghamshire that they finally confronted each other. The Parliamentarians led by John Hampden riding down from Golder Hill to Chalgrove Field, separated only by a hedge from the waiting Royalists led by Prince Rupert. There were to be many charges and desperate vicious fighting, but it was in the very first charge that John Hampden sustained serious injury and was

The statue of John Hampden which stands in Aylesbury's Market Square.

taken from the battlefield, first to his father-in-law's house at Pyrton Manor and then on to Ezekiel Browne's home, later to become the Greyhound Inn at Thame. To this day there is still a debate as to how he sustained his fatal wound. Was he shot in the shoulder by Royalists or did an overloaded pistol explode in his hand? The weight of evidence points to a fatal gunshot from the Royalists.

Such was Hampden's reputation as a man of integrity, that even the king was persuaded to offer his personal physician to try and save Hampden's life. But it was all in vain and just over a week later Hampden died. The date was the anniversary of his wedding to his beloved Elizabeth, 24th June 1643.

The Greencoats escorted his coffin to Hampden House, with hundreds of local people braving the dangerous war environment to pay their last respects to this true Buckinghamshire hero. His final resting place is his home village of Great Hampden in the Church of St Mary Magdalene.

The county still pays tribute to this local hero. In a poll run by the *Bucks Free Press* newspaper in 2002, John Hampden was awarded the title of 'Buckinghamshire's Greatest Person'. We can add to that 'and Buckinghamshire Hero'.

8

Dame Frances Dove (1847–1942)

'She could be terrifying and she could be charming.'

'When I was a girl, the chief ideas of the mothers of that day
appeared to be to give their daughters a superficial veneer of
French, drawing and music, then dress them up and hawk them
about, until a husband was dazzled and caught; and my whole
soul revolted against this degradation of womanhood.'
(Miss Frances Dove: *'The Modern Girl: How Far Are We Fitting Her
For Her Varied Duties In Life'* June 1907)

Miss Frances Dove was nothing, if not, forthright. The
above statement was made to a gathering of head-
mistresses in 1907, keen to hear the views of this still
pioneering 60-year-old educationalist – the much admired
woman who founded and managed the highly successful girls'
public school, Wycombe Abbey, in Buckinghamshire, just over a
decade earlier.

'Her silvery hair surmounts a still young face, a face lit up by
keen kindly eyes. She speaks with perfect self-command in public
as well as in private, quietly, sincerely and modestly, yet with the
distinction which comes of a well-stored and widely interested
mind.'

This verbal picture drawn by a *Daily Mail* journalist the
following year describes her perfectly. Indeed she had an
abundant quality of sternness expected of a renowned headmistress, but also a very soft side, particularly for charitable
causes that assisted in lifting the burden of poverty from young
children living in the unhealthy confines of London's East End.

The very first Head Girl of Wycombe Abbey, Ursula Townsend, described her '. . . great generosity and readiness to help anyone in need. She could be terrifying and she could be charming.'

Miss Dove was probably one of the foremost exponents of balancing that fine line between a radical determination to improve the lot of women through education – which she did – and yet, at the same time, remaining strategically tolerant of the inevitable prejudice women suffered during the Victorian and Edwardian era and beyond. Her achievement in founding and running Wycombe Abbey School and advancing the causes of women's education certainly qualify her for hero status.

Jane Frances Dove was born on 27th June 1847 during her parents' honeymoon in Bordeaux. Honeymoons at that time, for those who could afford them, were often turned into 'Grand European Tours' of a year or more, easily time for the happy couple to conceive and give birth to their first born, all in blissful wedlock. Indeed, John and Jane Dove moved on for another year to Spain before returning to Lincolnshire and then to a 'living' for her curate father in Marylebone, London.

Frances was the eldest of the Doves' ten children to be born, of whom six survived. By the time Frances was thirteen years old, she had experienced a rigorous home education, together with brothers Horace and Arthur. They were all taught by their father as well as a neighbour, who was able to instruct them in Hebrew and German. Already that would be a great deal more exposure to world knowledge than most young woman of that age and era, but as she entered her teenage years, her parents then arranged for her to attend Queen's College in London's Harley Street. This was a pioneering institution in itself, its goals being to instruct ladies to go on to become teachers. A student there for nearly three years, Frances was, both consciously and unconsciously, absorbing new era values about the worth of women and the importance of their further and higher education.

DAME FRANCES DOVE (1847-1942)

Frances Dove.
(by kind permission of Wycombe Abbey School)

Then, when she was fifteen, it all came down to earth with a bump. In 1862, her father, the Reverend John Thomas, was appointed to a new living as far removed from the modern ethos of London living and education as possible. The family moved to Cowbit, in Lincolnshire.

This, it could be said, gave Frances the other side of her nature. The practical, caring and understanding woman who, alongside proclaiming the social and educational advancement of girls, in her 1907 paper as a 60-year-old headmistress, also announced that the modern girls' chief duty '. . . is first to be a good daughter and secondly a good wife and mother'.

BUCKINGHAMSHIRE HEROES

*Frances Dove. This picture is thought to have
been taken in 1907. (by kind permission of
Wycombe Abbey School)*

And a good daughter she was. She took up her needle, making
the family's clothes and dutifully assisting her mother in running
the remote Lincolnshire household. This was a location where
rain-water became their drinking water, pumped by hand to the
house and where, it is claimed, home-grown food supplies were
supplemented by the occasional eel taken from a flooded ditch
or wild fowl shot by local farmers.

It was also very cold in the winter, the only high point being
the chance to enjoy ice-skating, an activity she much favoured for
her girls all those years later as headmistress of Wycombe Abbey
School. Was there in the daydreams of this fifteen-year-old girl
any inkling of that ambition to found and run her own school,
with plenty of vigorous and exciting recreation on the syllabus?

DAME FRANCES DOVE (1847–1942)

She found it more than just frustrating '. . . watering the cabbages and looking forward to the return of the boys for the holidays'. But she had more than glimpsed the other world; the world of further education and advancement for women beyond being a dutiful daughter and future mother. To her parents' credit, they also realized that Jane Frances Dove was frustrated by the drastic curtailment of access to educational avenues and her lack of further schooling. So she was admitted to a boarding school in Chiswick, obtaining yet more experience of independent living to inform her later role as headmistress of one of the most renowned Buckinghamshire boarding schools. However, the poor standard of education at this Chiswick school where some girls were forced to sleep two to a bed, for a not insignificant fee of £80 a year, saw her withdrawal after only one year learning 'everything a school ought not to be'.

It was at this time, in her teenage years, that she began to consider what could be made possible for young women to progress in matters of knowledge and world affairs. Provision for country girls in particular, as she was then, was so very poor and this infuriated her. Also, it seemed to her very unfair that her brothers were having such a great time at public school. Why should such efforts only be dedicated to the male of the species? Thus was born the theme that would strongly characterize her later determination to create her own public school for girls – not just on the image and model of the best of those for boys' schools, but much better, more caring, more lively and more fun.

It would take another 31 years of dedicated determination to realize her dream and create such a school in the Buckinghamshire countryside. The time between, shaped a woman of quite amazing character. Growing up in the era of the suffrage move-ment, as well as a major revolution in the provision of education for women, Frances was able to be part of that revolution by attending Benslow House in Hitchen, the forerunner of Girton

College, Cambridge, founded by Miss Emily Davies. As one of the 'Girton Pioneers', Frances took her scholarship exams in 1871 at Hitchen College but missed achieving an award.

In a personal letter to Miss Dove from Miss Davies on 28th June 1871, she said, 'You were first in Mathematics, but, as you expected, in Latin & in History, you came lower down. I hope it may be managed for you to come to the College tho' you have not gained a scholarship, as I feel that with good, regular teaching, you would get on well and do credit both to yourself & the College.'

In the event, it was one Jane Frances Dove, who laid claim to the honour of being the first pupil to cross the threshold of Girton College, Cambridge, in 1873.

Nothing, but nothing would have kept her away. The college was still in the throes of being built and true to her practical upbringing she spent her momentous first day at Girton cleaning the college windows. Working amongst cement barrels, heaps of bricks and with carpenters hammering away, and having to eat cold meals and with little heat and only candle light, this was a distant echo of things to come. She was also one of the first of two women in the history of women's higher education to sit for the Natural Sciences Tripos at Cambridge in 1874 and succeed.

One can only imagine what triumph she felt, as a young woman of 27 years of age, clutching her degree from Girton College, signed by its legendary founder. It was from that moment on, that she dedicated her life to the education of young women. Firstly as a science mistress at Cheltenham College, teaching physiology, then in 1877 at St Andrews School for Girls in Edinburgh, later to become St Leonards. She became headmistress there in 1882 at the relatively young age of 35. Her legendary development of that school is a separate story in its own right, but during her fourteen years at the helm, her desire to build her own school for girls from scratch became

DAME FRANCES DOVE (1847–1942)

overwhelming. It was with this desire in mind that she resigned in October 1895.

She said in her resignation letter, 'I take this step because I am possessed with the idea that the benefits which I believe to be conferred by this school should be more widely diffused, and that this may be done by founding one, or possible two or more sister schools.' This typifies her enthusiasm – spreading opportunities and possibly starting not one but two or even more avenues of education for women. She referred to this moment as one for her to 'try the new experiment myself'.

From that decision onwards, it was as if she had been re-born. With boundless energy and skilful perception, within two months of leaving her post at St Leonards in 1896, she had founded a brand new school for girls in High Wycombe. In this venture all the trials and tribulations she had encountered on her journey from teenager to mature academic leader were to stand her in good stead in what was an amazing achievement.

She began her 'experiment' in creating this new school by ensuring that it had the necessary financial security to be launched. With the assistance of her cousin, Francis Larkin, as company secretary, and whilst still completing her resignation notice at St Leonards, they created the Girls Education Company Limited. This aimed to raise capital of £30,000 in 3,000 shares of £10 each. The prospectus to potential shareholders explained that in this new school, '. . . the proposed system of education aims at doing for girls, with suitable modifications, what the existing great Public Schools do for boys'.

The next task was to find a location for this new school. Francis Larkin scoured as many available property details as he could, looking for Frances's 'Eldorado'. The search was for 'a site where there was the least rainfall, propinquity to a town. A large house, ample space for cricket and other sports, and a lake for swimming and other purposes'.

BUCKINGHAMSHIRE HEROES

◆◆◆

After intensive searching, Frances chose Lord Carrington's House, Wycombe Abbey, in Buckinghamshire. This was to be her 'Eldorado'. As soon as the contract to purchase was signed in May, two months before actual legal completion took place in the sum of £20,000, Miss Dove, with her unstoppable optimism, immediately issued a school prospectus designed to take her first pupils on 23rd September. Here is her description of that long-dreamed of goal now in her grasp – Wycombe Abbey School:

'High Wycombe is a pleasant town among the Chalk Downs and the Beech Woods of Buckinghamshire, thirty miles from London on the Maidenhead and Oxford Branch of the Great Western Railway. Wycombe Abbey is on the outskirts of the town; it is a large and commodious building situated within its own beautiful grounds of thirty acres, and has been most favourable reported on, both as to position and arrangements, by Dr W H Corfield, Professor of Hygiene in University College London. The Abbey is large enough to accommodate the Head Mistress, and some of her Assistants, and about a hundred girls.

For this purpose it will be divided into four Houses. Each House will be under a House Mistress and will have its own sitting rooms and dormitories and tables in the Dining Hall, but all will be under the immediate superintendence of the Head Mistress.

A Gymnasium and Workshop will be among the first necessaries to be provided, and the buildings already include a Hall 120 feet long with a floor properly laid for dancing.

The grounds include a lake, an avenue of limes, other fine trees, an extensive tennis lawn and abundant space for cricket pitches, hockey grounds, and a golf course.

The School is intended to provide for girls an education which, while moderate in cost and especially adapted to their requirements, shall be as complete on all its sides as that given to boys at the great Public Schools. The number of girls in the School is intended to be two hundred.'

DAME FRANCES DOVE (1847–1942)

Frances Dove's most cherished dreams were now written down and on their way to being realized. For under £100 per year per pupil she was offering parents educational and recreation experiences for their daughters, the like of which was not available elsewhere, at least not in quite the 'Dove' mould of doing things. Her school was to be like no other, and for the first arrivals, it certainly seemed that way but not necessarily for all the right reasons,

'Our occupation of House Studies was soon to be interrupted, and from room to room we were pursued by men fitting the electric light . . . and as we carried our candles and books into strange Studies, we hugged the thought of light which could be produced without matches, and which spilt no grease.'

It was déjà vu for Miss Dove, but for her 'Wycombe Abbey pioneers' a brief period of discomfort that would elicit little sympathy from their new headmistress. The stalwart batch of first pupils worked amongst the conversion work and in cold corners and corridors as Miss Dove relentlessly pursued her improvements. The important thing was that the school had opened its doors on time, with a staff of fifteen mistresses and 40 girls, and her dream had truly taken off. Often sacrificing her own salary to pay for improvements and essential work, such as cleaning out the lake at a cost of £2,000, the school grew from strength to strength and by 1899, Miss Dove was proud to announce her school was full – she had 210 pupils after three years of operation. It was called by some, '. . . the most wonderful school in England'.

What was, in retrospect, a quite rare and welcome achievement by Miss Dove, and at a very early stage in the school's life, was its connection with the real world outside the cosy walls of Wycombe Abbey. Miss Dove regularly involved her girls from the outset in setting up much awaited days out to the Abbey for city children attending Camberwell missionary schools in London's East End. For example, in June 1897 at the end of the school's very first year, it hosted a visit of 89 girls from the United Girls' Schools' Mission, Camberwell. The very first issue of the school's own magazine, *Wycombe Abbey Gazette*, described the scene as follows, 'They arrived at about a quarter to eleven, and Miss Dove and some of the girls brought them from the station. They were divided into parties of ten, and each party wore a different coloured ribbon; when they arrived inside the Rupert Gate, nine of us each took possession of a party, and with other helpers, arranged for the amusement of that party from then until 4 o'clock. To begin with, we seated them on the lawn under the trees, and gave them dinner.

For some, after that, it was quite difficult to get them to do anything but enjoy the grass; they thought the feeling of it was "so lovely", and took off their boots and stockings to enjoy it to the full. Most of them had never been in a train at all, or anywhere, in fact, excepting the streets quite close to where they lived, so that the day was one full of new experiences to them.'

New experiences were what Miss Frances Dove was renowned for. She had created a school with a new vision for young women, and went on to produce some profound contributions to educational theory, particularly that relating to the importance of sports. She didn't see why women should not experience cricket, and at Wycombe Abbey they did.

Cold winter days at Cowbit for the young Frances Dove at least had the excitement of ice skating on flooded Norfolk plains, so, why not introduce her girls at Wycombe Abbey to the joys of winter skating at Cockmarsh in nearby Bourne End.

'Let us have games of all kinds . . . Let us have lawn tennis, fives, bowls, croquet, quoits, golf, swimming, skating, archery, tobogganing, basket-ball, rounders, and hailes, as many of these as can be provided for, and some at one season of the year, others at another.'

DAME FRANCES DOVE (1847–1942)

Miss Dove used the opportunity to campaign to open all and every sport possible to girls in order make the wider point that she called 'acquiring corporate virtues'. She explained, 'Men acquire corporate virtues, not only at school and at college, but almost in every walk of life; whereas comparatively few women ever find themselves members of an organised profession, and the proportion, even of those who have the advantage of college life, is still exceedingly small'.

Miss Dove continued to follow her own example as a role model to her girls and became fully involved in local corporate affairs. Close association with the parish church was immediate and constant. In her later years she dedicated a stained glass window, designed by a St Leonards Senior. She was always to the fore raising money whether it was for the Melanesian Mission in the South Seas, or the United Girls School Mission in Camberwell, or to build a new church or a new school in High Wycombe. She is described as a prime mover in the raising of funds for St John's Church in Desborough Road and a Church of England School in Loakes Park. She inaugurated High Wycombe's Central Aid Society in 1906. This was a quite remarkable organization designed to assist invalid children, local girls unlucky enough to be confined to the workhouse, as well as giving rise to an Infant Welfare Centre and, to assist with the devastating problem of tuberculosis, a special dispensary.

She was Wycombe's one woman whirlwind, quite unique in her energy, inspiration, and practical delivery of a whole range of health and educational facilities for the local population. In addition, she became a governor of High Wycombe Royal Grammar School, High Wycombe Technical Institute and High Wycombe School for Girls. She was the first woman to be elected to High Wycombe's Town Council serving on the committees concerned with health and hospital provision as well as the free library service.

BUCKINGHAMSHIRE HEROES

In 1908, aged 61, she stood as a candidate for the mayor of High Wycombe. But it seems that High Wycombe was not ready to be honoured as the first town in the whole of England to have a woman mayor. Her defeat by two votes in the mayoral elections of 1908 was described by *The Times* as resulting from 'Factitious opposition stirred up at the last moment'. The *Bucks Free Press* was incensed at this snub to Miss Dove. They reported that, 'The distinction of being the only woman member of High Wycombe Town Council was marred by one of the most regrettable controversies in the civic history of the Borough. Dame Francis Dove was approached and consented to be nominated for the mayorality in 1907. Opposition had sprung up within the council almost on the eve of mayoral election day, and at the statutory meeting held for the purpose, controversy reached such a pitch that it was impossible to come to a decision. Another meeting was convened at which the nominated candidate was out-voted, defeated by a small minority.' Frances herself said, 'I did not seek the honour – it was thrust upon me and some of those who thrust it upon me were amongst those who voted against me.' This was one threshold she was not going to cross.

Miss Dove was forthright, and was formidable – possibly too much so for some, keeping to the old legacy where a 'mayoral corporate identity' was strictly male. She had, prior to her unexpected defeat, stood her corner against the existing mayor and his deputy in a town council meeting discussing the possible location of a farming colony for consumptive convalescents in High Wycombe. Her sense of concern for assisting invalids to get better in Wycombe's fresh air went strictly against the mayor's fear of such people bringing their germs to his town. This stalemate could have been the reason she was plotted against in the final days of the 1908 mayoral elections.

Frances continued her diligent service to the council until resigning in 1921 when she was appointed a Justice of the Peace

DAME FRANCES DOVE (1847–1942)

for the county. However, the biggest wrench was her resignation as headmistress of her own creation, Wycombe Abbey School, in 1911. She wanted the school to benefit from younger blood at the helm and she decided that the time had come, whilst the school was riding high in prestige. What she bequeathed in educational provision is incalculable. Certainly her creation of The Seniors, a self-governing organisation that flourishes as old pupils continue to spread her ideas and their own 'corporate' successes, plus bequeathing funds to assist others to do likewise is a great success today, as is Wycombe Abbey School which continues to top the educational leagues.

Retiring to live in Little Kimble, she dreamed of opening a Montessori school for young children but that got pushed to the back of a very busy life as she continued her work for the Town Council and the Judiciary. A familiar figure on her tricycle, in characteristic form, she took it upon herself to learn to drive at the age of 72. After all, new experiences were her hallmark. She also moved back to live in High Wycombe. In 1928 she was recognised for her long and remarkable contribution to education and local service, becoming a Dame Commander of the Order of the British Empire.

When Dame Frances Dove died in her High Wycombe home in Priory Avenue on Sunday 21st June 1942, a Buckinghamshire hero had been lost but a remarkable legacy established. At the time of her death, she was still the only woman to have been elected to High Wycombe Town Council.

That single fact speaks volumes for Frances Dove's strength of character, her pioneering spirit and the inevitable quest for new experiences as a role model for others to follow.

9

John Newton (1725–1807)

'All my plantations flourish.'

'It's impossible to know his story and not to wonder how he would feel if he were to be transported into the twenty-first century and hear the lines he wrote in his attic at Olney being sung on the street corners of London, in the folk clubs of New York, at the Brandenburg Gate in Berlin, on the mountainsides of Kenya, and in the secret churches of China; to hear the phrases he put together coming from the mouths of rock singers, mourners, anti-globalization protesters, and Christian worshippers of every denomination in every country in the world.' [Steve Turner: *Amazing Grace*, Lion, 2005, p.255]

Debauchery, depravity and the sheer depths to which man's inhumanity to man can sink form the foundation of John Newton's story. Remarkably, from such a foundation he emerges a hero, albeit a controversial one. As a former slave trader willingly dealing in the most appalling of human misery, he would never see himself as anything other than an infidel, a sinner of enormous magnitude. Yet in his Buckinghamshire attic in the town of Olney, from the volumes of writing he feverishly compiled between 1764 and 1779 as Olney's most famous curate, emerged the lines that Steve Turner acknowledges are known throughout the world, the hymn known simply as *Amazing Grace*. Indeed, its first appearance is in the publication known as the *Olney Hymns*, published in 1779, together with other works contributed by another of religious history's controversial figures, poet William Cowper.

JOHN NEWTON (1725–1807)

So it was that this small north Buckinghamshire market town based around the manufacture of straw plait and pillow lace-making became an intense focal point for a religious fervour and creative chemistry that was quite extraordinary. The people of Olney themselves are integral to the genesis of this most famous of songs and possibly these unnamed folk are the real Buckinghamshire heroes in this story.

Newton's creativity was directed specifically at them and for them, so *Amazing Grace* belongs in no uncertain terms to the people of that town.

It was the committed evangelist Lord Dartmouth, wealthy landowner and owner of the Great House in Olney, when seeking a clergyman for the parish church, who arranged for Newton's ordination as a Church of England priest and his position as curate. He knew Newton's story, that he was a former slave trader, a dealer, a sinner, a wretch who professed to having been saved by a miraculous religious conversion whilst navigating a storm at sea, subsequently turning to a life of religious servitude and evangelical preaching.

Its full detail, however, does not show a man who repented under stormy seas and relinquished the slave trade, but a flawed and some would say hypocritical man who continued in his disgusting trade, and, as he admitted, 'a slave to every customary vice'. In a case of poetic justice he, himself, fell victim to abuse and lived as a virtual slave on Plantain Island off the coast of the Sierra Leone. Additional humility was added to his plight as it was an African woman from the island's ruling Bombo family who owned him and starved him as she did her other slaves. So it was no sudden conversion, no overnight devil to angel but more of a slow drift that was to take years. There was never any real rejection of slavery. When he escaped his own shackles, he went back to work as a trader of human cargo. It was only a serious illness in 1755 that took him away from such seafaring.

BUCKINGHAMSHIRE HEROES

So when he arrived in Olney almost 20 years after his Plantain experience, a fervent evangelist and proclaimed infidel, he was bringing enormously complex mental anguish as his baggage which he would unpack in this small Buckinghamshire town. His wretchedness on Plantain, gave him the moral authority to talk of being saved. In the back of his mind perhaps the words that were one day to echo around the world were already forming,

> *Amazing grace! (how sweet the sound)*
> *That sav'd a wretch like me!*
> *I once was lost, but now am found,*
> *Was blind, but now I see.*

Unknown to the folk of Olney, Newton had just published his life

John Newton.

JOHN NEWTON (1725–1807)

story from his childhood in London's East End to his religious salvation, called *The Authentic Narrative*, when their 39-year-old, newly appointed curate and his 36-year-old wife Mary arrived in their town in 1764. The lacemakers, farmers and farm labourers, straw plaiters, stable hands, blacksmiths, carpenters, old and young, the poor and the vagrants, in all, a population of around 2,500, would judge and learn about their new curate by other means.

Learn they did. They learnt that he was a man of incredible passion and commitment to evangelical Christianity, especially in the form of hymns which came tumbling out of his religious creativity in Olney's supportive atmosphere. He thrived on public interaction and the people didn't let him down. After his first year he wrote, 'Congregation large and serious. Almost every week I hear of some either awakened or seriously impressed. We have now fixed a little company who come to my house on the Sabbath after tea. We spend an hour or more in prayer and singing and part between six and seven.'

He would also run special meetings for children, others for 'young and inquiring persons' and yet other meetings for the 'more experienced and judicious'. He travelled all around the hamlets nearby, passionately preaching and encouraging the singing of hymns, proclaiming, 'All my plantations flourish'.

Olney's parish church became so crowded that an additional gallery had to be added to house the expanding congregation. Newton was not only stimulated by the obvious participation of the local population and many out-of-town visitors who enjoyed his style and message, but by the arrival of the poet William Cowper.

Cowper was to inject into Newton a fervour of hymn writing that did literally, spill over into Cowper's insanity and feed his long-standing persecution complex that he was incapable of God's forgiveness. Even God plotted against him. Cowper arrived in Olney, not only having been treated for periods of insanity, but during his calmer times, having formed a deep relationship with the wife of the Reverend Morely Unwin of Huntington. When the Reverend Unwin met with a fatal horse-riding accident, it freed the way for Cowper to take Mary Unwin with him away from the Huntington gossip. So she also arrived in Olney and both being temporarily in need of shelter, they stayed with John Newton before renting Orchard Side, on Market Place, close to the vicarage.

So began the Cowper-Newton partnership, with Newton setting himself a target of writing a new hymn every week to feed their regular special meetings now held in Lord Dartmouth's Great Room at the Great House. Upwards of 130 people could be accommodated and demands to be present at a Cowper-Newton double act, whether at the parish church or at the Great Room afterwards, could easily exceed this, running to possibly 200 people seeking entry. Newton even took to issuing tickets, 'to exclude some who only come to look about them'.

During 1767, the year that William Cowper and Mary Unwin arrived in Olney, John Newton published his *Olney Sermons*. Also, he was soon to publish a *Review of Ecclesiastical History* (1770). Meanwhile both Cowper and Newton were writing hymns for the people of Olney. Steve Turner's research for his study *Amazing Grace*, pinpoints this legendary hymn, penned by Newton in that Olney vicarage attic room, to the second half of December 1772, although no one knows what it would have sounded like when first aired in the Great Room shortly afterwards. Newton only wrote the words and was not a musician. Meanwhile, Cowper was falling back into melancholy and it appeared insanity was returning and he ceased writing around 1773.

When the *Olney Hymns* were finally published in February 1779, the 428-page book contained 68 written by Cowper and 280 written by Newton. *Amazing Grace*, Hymn 41, had the listed title, 'Faith's Review and Expectation.' Unfortunately, Cowper was never to concede that he was capable of God's forgiveness and could not accept Newton's belief expounded by this hymn of repentance and forgiveness. Some claim that apart from reflecting Newton's conversion to Christianity from his sinful life; it also had words aimed to console his good friend William Cowper.

The publication of the *Olney Hymns* marked the end of this remarkably productive era of passionate evangelical chemistry and creativity at Olney. Cowper was now seriously ill and died the following year. Newton moved on to accept the benefice of St Mary Woolnorth with St Mary in Woolchurch, Lombard Street, London. His wife, Mary, died of cancer on 15th December 1790 and his grief became insurmountable. His deep love was shown to the world when he published *Letters to a Wife* in 1793. He had been a prolific letter writer during all the years he spent at sea. John Newton died on 21st December 1807, to be buried with his wife at St Mary Woolnorth. Their remains were transferred to Olney in 1893.

Myllar & Owen's *Dictionary of National Biography* (1921/2) comments of his letters, 'He unfolded the innermost recesses of his life-long love. He had no dread of the world's judgment which leads most men to shrink from uttering their darkest and holiest secrets.' He didn't shrink from judgement – he sought out judgment and in a Buckinghamshire attic he found grace, Amazing Grace and gave that back to the world.

Does that make him a Buckinghamshire hero? You decide.

10

Geoffrey Palmer OBE

Actor

'If there's a gentle smile . . . that's the nicest thing.'

Many 'gentle smiles' are directed towards our last county hero, smiles associated with pleasure and good memories. The constant flickers of recognition that Geoffrey Palmer encounters exude a warmth of 'here is someone I know, someone I like'. Of course, if you are in the public eye, if you are a well-known professional actor, such recognition comes with the territory, but in Geoffrey's case he has carved himself a unique international persona as well as a special local relationship with Buckinghamshire and the Great Missenden area where he has lived for the last 43 years.

The magic of Roald Dahl's stories and rhymes that began our tour of county heroes come full circle when they encounter the additional ingredients of Geoffrey Palmer's voice and acting skills as he brings the BFG and so many other tales, stories and plays to audio life. This is the other powerful and highly recognisable quality that he holds and uses to perfection – his voice. Flickers of recognition occur in exactly the same way on hearing his warm, controlled, perfectly pitched tones that guide us through the television world of *Grumpy Old Men* or famously lending his articulate, clipped British tones to the German language to inform us about Audi cars and 'Vorsprung durch Technik.'

Geoffrey Palmer is a comfortable presence in so many people's lives. For many he is, and now always will be, Lionel Hardcastle romancing Jean (Judi Dench) in *As Time Goes By;* for others he'll

GEOFFREY PALMER OBE (BORN 1927)

Geoffrey Palmer.

always be Ben Parkinson, father to Russell and Adam and husband to Ria (Wendy Craig – *Butterflies*). Yet others recall the hapless Jimmy, brother-in-law to Reginald Perrin (Leonard Rossiter – *The Fall and Rise of Reginald Perrin*).

Or do you miss the batty Major Harry Kitchener Wellington Truscott, (*Fairly Secret Army*) or look forward to meeting Admiral Roebuck again as he and 'M' (Judi Dench) deal with a belligerent James Bond (*Tomorrow Never Dies*)? A very long list indeed is possible here but before such a list of credited performances began its genesis, Geoffrey Palmer's own entry to the world was on 4th June 1927 in North Finchley, a companion for his three-year-old brother.

As you explore Geoffrey's early life with him, it becomes clear that he could well have followed a military career of some kind. At Highgate School he ended up as Captain of Shooting, claiming it was the only thing he was very good at unless you count the award of a 'really naff' dictionary of quotations for 'the reading in chapel prize'.

As a teenager he aspired to what he regarded as the glamour of the Fleet Air Arm but at the medical discovered he was marginally colour blind so that avenue was closed off. In the event, by 1946, he had opted for the Marines as an HO (Hostilities Only) recruit reporting to 928 Squad at Deal. He looks back on this time, not with misplaced nostalgia, but with a real affection that not only did he enjoy being a Royal Marine, he was also quite good at it. Indeed, his talent for shooting, which had won him accolades at school, came into its own as he undertook

Geoffrey Palmer as a recruit for the Marines in 1946.

GEOFFREY PALMER OBE (BORN 1927)

a small arms instructor course and eventually was promoted to full Corporal Instructor.

In 1948, as an NCO, he left the Service, receiving a special grant given to ex-servicemen for re-training in 'Civvy Street'. In Geoffrey's case this involved something to do with Dutch baked beans and Swedish salad cream in an import-export business but more importantly, he confided , 'I just spent the time looking at the girls and thinking, "Oh gosh, I wish I were brave enough to ask them out"'. This ex-corporal instructor, now trainee business man, but hopelessly shy when it came to dating, was still living with his parents in North Finchley. He did break through his shyness enough to have a girlfriend and it is to her that credit must go for introducing Geoffrey Palmer to the acting profession he was to make so much his own.

Whilst he enjoyed the world of the local Woodside Park Players, his disillusionment with the business world was growing. He recalls, 'The girlfriend had got me into the local amateur dramatic society around this time and I suddenly thought one day, I really cannot do this bean rubbish anymore. I was 21 or 22 and had no interest in trying to sell Dutch baked beans and I remember thinking I'd better go and see the personnel manager, Mr Ritter. So I spoke to his secretary, it was a Friday I remember, and I said I'd like to see Mr Ritter. "What's it about?" she demanded, "Well I think I want to leave", I said, "I'll see if he's free", and I went in.

"Yes Palmer. What is it?"

"I want to leave sir."

"What are we paying you?"

"Five pounds a week sir."

"Suppose we give you seven?"

And I thought, "You s**t. If I was worth seven why didn't you give me seven last year?" I said "No thank you" and I left.'

He drifted a little, helping an accountant friend but that was not his forte, 'I couldn't add up or anything.' He persevered with the amateur dramatics, discovering to his amazement that some people actually made a living out of being an actor. He also found it was very pleasurable to experience people laughing and clapping at the end of a performance. He was hooked.

So in his early 20s, he placed his foot on the first rung of his theatrical ladder, landing a job with the Q Theatre on the north side of Kew Bridge.

The catch was that he was an *unpaid* trainee assistant manager. Surviving for around a year he did achieve waged status of about £3 a week or so before moving on to the Grand Theatre, Croydon, as an assistant stage manager. Locating props and playing incidental parts, his theatrical apprenticeship steadily progressed until he was taken into the repertory company as 'juvenile character'. He began working in rep e.g. Leatherhead, Canterbury, Guilford, Aberdeen, Glasgow and Edinburgh, building a reputation by his mid 20s as a 'youngish leading man'.

Despite having a 'grotty agent', right time, right place, right age did work in Geoffrey's favour as his theatrical training was ideal for the new doors opening in commercial television around the mid-1950s.

At this time, Geoffrey was sharing a sparse flat 'at the wrong end of Chelsea', close to Granada's London studios, so picked up lots of bits and pieces with them. He also worked for ATV, when they had the Wood Green Empire and the Hackney Empire, before they were at Elstree. He worked with some of the top variety shows and comedians of that time such as Arthur Askey, Harry Worth, Dickie Valentine and his own hero, Jimmy James. His famous career as a voice-over artist could be said to have started at that time also, when he was given 'out of vision' announcements:

'*From the North, Granada presents, THE ARMY GAME, starring Michael Medwin, William Hartnell, Alfie Bass......etc. etc.*'

GEOFFREY PALMER OBE (BORN 1927)

He loved working on *The Army Game*, apart from the fact that the studio was 500 yards from his flat, and it ran for over four years. Geoffrey fondly recalls, 'I got seven guineas for nothing – for half a minute's work every Friday night and then I'd do something for the odd quiz show – I was the local, cheap, jack-of-all-trades.'

What really got him closer to being in front of the television cameras was his job on *The Alan Young Show* around 1957.

Geoffrey explains, 'Alan Young wasn't happy the way the show was shot when they did the first one – so he wanted someone (this was live television as well) to act his part in the dress rehearsal of the two main sketches – brilliantly funny sketches – that made up the show. He wanted someone to do what he did on camera so he could watch it to see if the camera shots were right and decide what he thought should be a close up. So that was my job. I did what he did on the rehearsal and then I was finished. But again, being around, I did the 'out of vision' announcement *"From the North, Granada, It's The Alan Young Show, starring Alan Young, Petula Clarke our guest star this week"* (or Pearl Carr and Teddy Johnson) or whoever it was. It wasn't because I had a wonderful voice, I just happened to be there.'

Sorry, Geoffrey – the voice cannot be discounted so easily. His television commercial work has become legendary. The pitch, diction, shading and richness of his voice, honed by thousands of hours of acting was excellent then, and is certainly first-class now, and still puts him at the very top of the country's voice-over artists. Although way back in 1984, the Audi car advertisement is still something totally associated with him. 'A German lady who lived opposite', recalled Geoffrey, 'said it was a pity that everyone talked about that commercial, "This is very silly," she said, "because Geoffrey does not pronounce it correctly" – totally missing the point!'

Geoffrey's theatrical career and television work continued

apace during the 1960s when he was winning parts in some of the legendary series of that decade: *Police Surgeon*; *The Avengers*; *The Saint*; *Top Secret*; *Out of the Unknown*; *Z-Cars*; *Paul Temple*; *Dr Who*; and many many more were collected along the way. However, one series in particular had another significance for him. It was a series for Granada called *Family Solicitor*, and it was, while staying in digs, he met the woman he was to fall in love with. Still a shy, quiet man, he did pluck up the courage to propose to and marry Sally Green in 1963. That same autumn, they moved to Buckinghamshire, the county they have loved and lived in ever since.

Geoffrey continued to become more and more sought after for television work – his face now very recognizable, even if the name was still one yet to be more firmly established in people's minds. His work in the 1970s, however, soon put that right. In 1971, John Osborne cast him in his play *West of Suez* at the Royal Court, and Lindsay Anderson grabbed him for a key role as the doctor in his hit film *O Lucky Man* (1973). But for Geoffrey, it was a telephone call to his Buckinghamshire home in 1974 that really confirmed he had arrived. The call was from Sir Laurence Olivier who offered him a part in his National Theatre production of J.B.Priestley's play, *Eden End*. He didn't audition him as he knew he wanted Geoffrey Palmer to play Priestley's Geoffrey Farrant in this plot of family under-currents, which he did to great acclaim. Other substantial parts with legendary actors were on the cards, so whatever else he went on to achieve he ended up not only working for Sir Laurence Oliver, but with, and for, Sir John Gielgud, Paul Scofield and Sir Ralph Richardson. 'Not a bad bunch to work with, is it?' he reflects.

The fame that was to come his way, though, did not rest in his highly regarded theatrical performances, but as one of television's favourite sit-com stars. This began in the mid 1970s with *The Fall and Rise of Reginald Perrin*, and the role of Jimmy.

GEOFFREY PALMER OBE (BORN 1927)

However, it may never have been, as Geoffrey explains, 'John Howard Davies directed the pilot – the first one they did – and the pilot worked so then they commissioned a whole series. But Jimmy didn't appear in the first one and I did not know John Howard Davies – so if Jimmy had appeared in the pilot, someone else would have got the job. Then my career would have been very, very different.'

Geoffrey knew Gareth Gwenlan who directed the series, as he had previously worked on some pilots with him, written by Carla Lane and by Michael Frayn. After the first series of *Fall and Rise*, Gareth came down to Geoffrey's Buckinghamshire home with another Carla Lane script to show him and that was *Butterflies*. 'So it is very much a toss of the coin.'

I have refrained (until now) from mentioning what have become almost obligatory and usually first line introductory descriptions of Geoffrey's face. It is very personal to refer to someone as lugubrious, to refer to their hangdog countenance or blood-hound looks, or see them as having an archetypal middle-class, possibly slightly dull, down-trodden husband expression (whatever that may be). Sue Lawley began a recent *Desert Island Discs* with the words, 'His mournful expression and rich voice have made him a household name.'

These descriptions and many more abound but not with the taint of insult but affection, and, as his sit-com fame increased, so did the ways of describing him. When we spoke of this, he did seem to have a sneaking preference for one piece that began, 'The rugged, craggy face that has often dominated our television screens in recent years.'

Can you be rugged, craggy and lugubrious? I'm not sure but in the final analysis, he has an actor's face – one of expression and interest that holds the viewers, theatre audiences, and film-goers. He has a voice that similarly compels listening attention and a superb acting talent that sees him range from Trollope to

BUCKINGHAMSHIRE HEROES

Geoffrey Palmer wearing a Care2Wear wristband in support of the work of the Iain Rennie Hospice at Home.

Shakespeare to Dickens and Priestly on the one hand, and to John Cleese, Carla Lane, David Nobbs and Bob Larbey on the other. It was no surprise, except to Geoffrey, that his 'Services to the Theatre' were rewarded in the 2005 honours list with an OBE.

His role as Lionel Hardcastle, romancing Jean in *As Time Goes By* has scored quite an astounding following. In some cases, as in America, this is their first introduction to Geoffrey Palmer, British actor. For American ladies of a certain age who fantasize about being Judi Dench, they have dedicated websites and they even meet for 'Lionel Hardcastle lunches'.

Of course Lionel is never there but imagine the scene should one Geoffrey Palmer happen to call by – ambulances would need to be on stand-by. Geoffrey is more realistic about *As Time Goes By*, 'You would think it was Bertrand Russell or something the way people talk about it – I know it is not. I think it is a very clever situation comedy – end of story. That's all there is.'

GEOFFREY PALMER OBE (BORN 1927)

Geoffrey's celebrity status does not sit as easily on his shoulders as one might imagine. For him, his job happens to be that of an actor, albeit now a very successful and well-known one who is very much part of the local Buckinghamshire scene – a local celebrity, of course, but the label is not of his choice, it just comes with the territory. Had he not been Geoffrey Palmer, actor, he quite fancied his hand at farming – not so many 'gentle smiles' in farming and probably not so many requests to support good causes and turn-up at local events – something he does with a refreshing frankness. Commenting on a recent charity wristband campaign for the local Iain Rennie Hospice at Home, for which he is patron, he explained to me, 'If they want publicity, they've got a better chance of doing it if they have a quasi-celeb, otherwise the *Bucks Free Press*, or the *Gazette* or the *Herald* won't turn up at all. I don't do much.'

Geoffrey does have a friendly, accessible character that endears him to his local community, and it is the same accessibility he would extend to anyone whom he felt he could assist: a willingness to turn up, be Geoffrey Palmer – (we might see Lionel or Jimmy or Ben – that's up to us), and bring publicity and attention to the cause in hand. He doesn't do much – he's just Geoffrey Palmer, OBE, actor and Buckinghamshire Hero.

Bibliography

Adair, John, *John Hampden: A Memorial*. The Hampden Lectures, Market Group Management, 1993

Bowerman, Elsie, *Stands There A School: Memories of Dame Frances Dove*. Dolphin Press, 1965

Dahl, Felicity and Roald, *Memories With Food at Gipsy House*. Viking, 1991

Dahl, Roald, *Boy*. Jonathan Cape, 1984

Dahl, Roald, *My Year*. Jonathan Cape, 1993

Dahl, Roald, *The BFG*. Puffin, 1984

Eaton Griffith, Valerie, *A Stroke in the Family*. Wilwood House, 1970

Hansford-Miller, Frank, *John Hampden of Buckinghamshire – The People's Hero*. The John Hampden Society, 1997

Houghton, John, *Historic Figures in the Buckinghamshire Landscape*. The Book Castle, 1997

Mills, John, *Up In The Clouds Gentlemen Please*. Orion Books, 2001

Simons, Andrew, *Black British Swing:The African Diaspora's Contribution to England's Own Jazz of the 1930s and 1940s*. Northway Publications, 2005

Smith, Michael, *Station X*. Pan Books, 2004

Treglown, Jeremy, *Roald Dahl*. Faber and Faber, 1994

Turner, Steve, *Amazing Grace*. Lion Hudson, 2005

Verney, Margaret M, *Bucks Biographies*. Claridon Press, 1912

Williamson, Lori, *Rural Robustness – health and medicine in the nineteenth-century countryside*. Berks FHS Family Historian, Sept. 2001.

Index

BUCKINGHAMSHIRE HEROES